A TEEN BIBLE STUDY BASED O—

# RUN THE RACE

## TREY BRUNSON & JAKE McENTIRE

LifeWay Press®
Nashville, Tennessee

**STUDENT MINISTRY PUBLISHING**

**Ben Trueblood**
*Director, Student Ministry*

**John Paul Basham**
*Manager, Student Ministry Publishing*

**Karen Daniel**
*Editorial Team Leader*

**Stephanie Livengood**
*Content Editor*

**Jeff Belcher**
*Content Editor*

**Jennifer Siao**
*Production Editor*

**Amy Lyon**
*Graphic Designer*

ISBN: 978-1-4627-9495-9
Item Number: 005802009

Dewey Decimal Classification Number: 234
Subject Heading: Christianity / Salvation and Grace

Printed in the United States of America.

Student Ministry Publishing
LifeWay Resources
One LifeWay Plaza
Nashville, TN 37234

We believe that the Bible has God for its author; salvation for its end; and truth, without any mixture of error, for its matter and that all Scripture is totally true and trustworthy. To review LifeWay's doctrinal guideline, please visit www.lifeway.com/doctrinalguideline. Unless otherwise noted, all Scripture quotations are taken from the Christian Standard Bible®, Copyright ©2017 by Holman Bible Publishers. Used by permission. Christian Standard Bible® and CSB® are federally registered trademarks of Holman Bible Publishers.

# [CONTENTS]

# ABOUT THE AUTHORS

**TREY BRUNSON** has served as a pastor in Texas, Florida, and California, and he currently serves as the Director of Communications for Southeast Christian Church in Louisville, Kentucky. He was an Executive Producer for *Run the Race* with his best friend and creator of the movie, Jake McEntire. He feels called to chase the next generation with the hope of the gospel because of God's gracious work in his life as a high school student. He earned his bachelor's degree from Dallas Baptist University where he also met his wife, Rachael, and his best friend, Jake. From there he served on staff at First Baptist Church Dallas, First Baptist Church Jacksonville where he was ordained, then he planted Story City Church in Burbank, California, and served on staff at Crossings Ministries before coming on staff at Southeast Christian Church. He is currently working on his Master of Divinity in Biblical Counseling at The Southern Baptist Theological Seminary. He is married to his amazing wife, Rachael, and they are blessed to be the parents of Wyatt Bear McCall (5), Judah Knox (3), Scout Helena (1), and their newborn son, Rivers Haddon.

**JAKE McENTIRE** is a passionate actor, writer, and producer. He is a graduate of Dallas Baptist University where he first wrote the screenplay for *Run the Race*. While there he met his best friend Trey Brunson, who would become his ministry partner and an Executive Producer on the movie. Together they feel called to encourage people, especially the youth of America, to run after Jesus Christ as the giver and meaning of all life. They believe one of the best ways to do this is through powerful stories and film. Still a resident of North Texas, Jake is a member of The Village Church in Flower Mound, Texas, where he has served as a homegroup leader. He's been married to his lovely wife, Charity, since 2007 and together they have one son, John "Silas" McEntire (1).

# NOTE FROM THE AUTHOR

I will never forget the day I met Jake. We were in the same spiritual disciplines class at Dallas Baptist University, and when the professor dropped a bad joke, we were the only two who laughed. After that class, we connected and quickly became best friends. Over the next four years, I heard Jake talk about an idea for a movie. I finally told him I never wanted to hear him talk about the idea again, because if he didn't start writing a script, no one would see the movie and it wouldn't matter. Next thing I knew, he handed me almost 200 pages of a script.

What you will see on whatever screen you watch this movie on, is the answer to over 10,000 prayers. Jake and I walked with this story for over fourteen years before God finally allowed us to share it with you. It's a miracle that we made the movie, and we pray for it to be a catalyst for many more miracles. The Lord gave us fourteen years of waiting and three years of working on this movie to sift our hearts and make sure we really believed the message we wrote and filmed. We want you to know Jesus is better than anything in this world. Life can be overwhelmingly difficult, but that doesn't mean God isn't there or isn't doing something very good. We hope the movie helps students and their parents see this story (largely based off true stories) and be encouraged that they can trust God. *You can trust God.*

As for this book, we pray that students will walk through the content and clearly know the gospel. You need to know who God is, who you are, what Jesus has done, and what that means for you and the rest of the world. The six sessions in this book are a gospel presentation of sorts. Packed inside those sessions are some of the most important truths the Lord has allowed me to learn and grow in. Student ministers, I pray that this would be a weapon to help you fight for the next generation's hearts. Student ministry leaders and volunteers, I pray this helps you understand and communicate the most amazing story about God's love for you and the students you pour into. Students, I pray this book points you to how big God is and how big God's love for you is. Jesus can change everything in your life. Nothing has been the same in my life since I surrendered to Jesus. God not only has a plan for your life to bring Him glory, but He has also designed things to bring you serious amounts of joy. Jesus is enough, and I pray this study helps you see His excellency, supremacy, and crazy love for you.

To the praise of His glory,

*Trey Brunson*

# INTRODUCTION

What do you think of when you hear the words *Run the Race*? You may think of the 100-yard dash in the Olympics, a long cross-country marathon, an extensive journey, or the span of one's life. The words *Run the Race* can bring many different situations to mind, but they are all associated with movement from one place to another. Every race has a starting point, then the gun sounds and you venture out to the finish line. You gradually leave one place and arrive at another.

In writing the story and screenplay for *Run the Race,* I wanted to show a person on a journey, running after his dreams and everything else he thinks might bring him happiness and joy. He's running only to discover it's impossible to get the most joy out of life apart from the One who made joy and life. The old saying is, "Life is about the journey, not the destination, so enjoy the journey." This type of thinking will leave you empty and discouraged because you are relying on your circumstances to bring you comfort and peace. You're relying on your own will to white knuckle a smile and act like everything is okay. Let's be honest, sometimes the journey is horrible with no end in sight. Sometimes the pain of life is overwhelming, and you wish you could make it all go away. Are you just supposed to enjoy the journey then?

Our goal for anyone who sees the movie or participates in this study is that you would learn to look to Jesus, understand that God made you in His image for a relationship with Him, and know that your purpose can only be found in Him. The life He gave you is your race with a start and end point. The race will be filled with many ups and downs, but no matter what your life journey brings you, if you can find your identity, purpose, and joy in Jesus Christ, then you have made it. At that point, you have won your race, and you will eventually spend eternity in the presence of the living God.

*Run the Race* isn't about enjoying the journey, but finding and looking to Jesus Christ during your journey, enjoying Him no matter what happens to you. It's about knowing that if you have Him, you have everything you'll ever need.

*Run the Race* has been a 14-year mission for me and my best friend, Trey Brunson. The journey has been painful at times, but God has also given us some unbelievable, miraculous stories of happiness. Either way, it has motivated us to press in and run after Jesus a little bit more each day, relying on Him for our salvation, purpose, peace, and overall joy. We pray that you'll be encouraged to do the same.

God bless,

*Jake McEntire*

# HOW TO USE

*Run the Race* is an six-session study to help your students understand the power of and the importance of sharing the gospel, while equipping them to share their faith with their friends. Prior to beginning this study, we encourage you to set aside time to watch the feature film, *Run the Race*, with students.

The study consists of four main elements: watch, discuss, apply, and on your own.

## WATCH

Each session contains video clips from the *Run the Race* movie as well as a summary of how those clips apply to that session's lesson.

## DISCUSS

This section digs deeper into the main theme of the video with cultural and biblical examples and questions.

## APPLY

Building on the Discuss section, Apply breaks down Scripture to help students learn how to walk out what they've learned through the group study. This section contains Scripture reading and summaries, as well as questions for deeper growth.

## ON YOUR OWN

This section contains three days of personal study. These studies are built to help students continue to connect with what they learned in the group session throughout the week.

## LEADER GUIDE

In the back of this book, we've provided tips, suggestions, and bonus content to help leaders as they walk through the study with their students.

> *"Therefore since we also have such a large cloud of witnesses surrounding us, let us lay aside every weight and the sin that so easily ensnares us, and run with endurance the race that lies before us, keeping our eyes on Jesus, the source and perfecter of our faith, who for the joy that lay before Him endured a cross and despised the shame, and has sat down at the right hand of God's throne."*
>
> **HEBREWS 12:1-2**

# WE ALL HAVE A PLAN, BUT GOD...

PROVERBS 16:9

## WATCH

In this scene, we see Dave and Zach celebrating the good news that the University of Florida is interested in Zach. It's in this moment of celebration that we see a plan being formed. Zach has wanted to get out of Bessemer for a long time, and now he has found the way. He has a "plan."

## DISCUSS

Do you have a plan for your life? Your plan could be to go to college, get married, become a doctor, lawyer, or maybe a barista at Starbucks. Maybe you're the kind of person who plans the entire day, or maybe you're the kind of person who just plans to enjoy whatever the day throws at you. We all have a tendency to try to create and control our future. The problem is that none of us can control what happens next.

**How do you try to plan and control your life?**

For instance, I love to spend time outdoors, particularly backpacking. Who doesn't enjoy sitting around a campfire with friends, making s'mores? One of the first (and most important) rules campers learn is: Make sure the fire is completely out! Here's a simple "how-to": Drown the campfire with water. Scrape all glowing embers off sticks that were burning. Stir the coals and water together. Then add more water!

The problem is, many people don't take this seriously enough, and from time to time, a spark remains. Then, the wind blows just right and carries the ember to dry leaves, and *whoosh!* Someone's carelessness turns into tragedy for many.

**What happens when your plans don't go the way you hoped?**

In 2017, wildfires spread across the western U.S. and scorched more than 66 million acres, destroying thousands of homes and killing dozens of people. It's possible one large fire in Oregon was started by teens playing with firecrackers. *Firecrackers!* They'd likely planned to have a little innocent fun, but something so small, harmless, and seemingly under control turned out to be completely devastating.

Have you ever felt like things were out of control in your life? We all make plans—that's normal and healthy. But what do we do when things don't go as planned? Zach and Dave's plan is probably not so different from some plans you've made in your life. Proverbs 16:9 tells us that we can make plans, but ultimately the Lord is the One in control of our lives, and that's definitely a good thing!

**Describe a time you set a goal you failed to achieve.**

**What does it look like to submit to God's plan instead of making your own?**

## PLANNING OR SUBMITTING—THE STORY OF JOSEPH

We all have goals and dreams for our lives. In some sense, this is vital, because we need direction and vision. But we can all be tempted to control our lives in unhealthy ways. Here's a perfect example: How many unedited pictures are on your social media feeds, how many have the perfect filter, and how much time have you spent polishing your image? That's control. If not achieving one of your goals would be crushing, you might have an issue with control. We all have this dangerous tendency of thinking we are in control of our lives, when in reality, we can control very little.

**When have you believed you were in control of something in your life only to have that very situation spiral out of control completely?**

No one struggled with this more than one of the first major characters in the Bible: Joseph. Genesis has two parts—the creation of the world (Gen. 1-11) and the creation of the nation of Israel (Gen. 12-50). The second part is broken into four smaller parts, each focusing on one of four men: Abraham (Gen. 12-25), Isaac (Gen. 25-26), Jacob (Gen. 27-36), and Joseph (Gen. 37-50). Joseph is one of the fathers of Israel, and God gave him a dream as a young boy. He dreamed twice that his brothers would bow down to him and that he would rule over them. Of course, Joseph decided to tell all his brothers about his dream.

If you have a brother or sister, you can probably guess what happened next. Joseph's brothers didn't respond well to hearing about a dream where they bowed before their brother. In fact, they were enraged. To make it worse, Joseph was their father's favorite, and Israel (their father) gave him a special coat. Because Joseph had the coat and the dreams, his brothers hated him so much they couldn't even muster a kind word to him.

One day while his brothers were out working, Joseph's father sent him to check on them and the sheep. As God revealed in the dream, Joseph would rule one day, but he'd been pampered and became prideful. He was exercising control in a way God hadn't designed it. As a result, Joseph wound up in a pit.

## APPLY

### Life in the Pit (Gen. 37)

What things are under your control? Can you make tomorrow happen? Can you keep your heart beating while you sleep? Can you ensure that a semitruck won't run you off the road on the way to work or school in the morning? As best as I can see it, I can only control my attitude and my response to what happens. Each one of us attempts to control our lives, from social media to our futures. From a biblical perspective, only One person is in control, and that is God. He simply spoke the world into being, and He continues to make happen the things He wants to happen. Daily, we struggle with control, and this reveals something profound—none of us is God. I'm not, and you're not. We can try to make things happen, if we don't learn that we aren't God and we can't control things, we'll end up in a pit like Joseph.

**How do you try to control your life? What are you trying to control right now?**

**Knowing God is in control, what changes will you make?**

### Life in the Prison (Gen. 39-40)

Joseph didn't stay in the pit, though. His brothers sold him into slavery, and despite his plan to rule, he wound up as a servant. He worked for Potiphar, who was an officer of Pharaoh in Egypt. While there, Joseph was accused falsely and imprisoned; it was as if he couldn't get any lower. From the pit to the prison, Joseph seemed to be spiraling down. Realizing we cannot control our lives can be a dizzying experience. Joseph was shaken, and he wound up far from home, in a desperate place, with no ability to control or change his circumstances. When Joseph could do nothing he learned something powerful. He was not God—but God is God, and He was at work bringing His plans to reality.

Joseph was essentially dead to those who loved him and forgotten by those who knew him, but God showed up. Two men were sent to the prison, the king's baker and cup-bearer, and Joseph was assigned to care for them. When Joseph heard these men had dreams they didn't understand, he proclaimed, "Don't interpretations belong to God?" (Gen. 40:8). While Joseph could not control his life, he could not stop God's plan for his life either. Joseph learned that no matter where he was, God is God and God is in control.

**When have you felt like your life was out of control? How can remembering that God is in control bring comfort?**

God used this situation to get him out of prison and bring him before Pharaoh, because Pharaoh also had a dream.

*"Pharaoh said to Joseph, 'I have had a dream, and no one can interpret it. But I have heard it said about you that you can hear a dream and interpret it.' 'I am not able to,' Joseph answered Pharaoh. 'It is God who will give Pharaoh a favorable answer.*
**GENESIS 41:15-16**

God showed up again and proved that He was in control and had a plan for Joseph's life.

## Life in the Palace (Gen. 41)

As Joseph began to realize God was in control and had a plan, He submitted to God and saw that God was doing something profoundly greater than he could have ever imagined. Joseph's original dream was that his brothers were bowing down to him. If you have siblings, you know this is a pretty amazing dream—but it was far too small.

*"So Pharaoh said to Joseph, 'Since God has made all this known to you, there is no one as discerning and wise as you are. You will be over my house, and all my people will obey your commands. Only I, as king, will be greater than you.'"*
**GENESIS 41:39-40**

Joseph went from a prisoner to the second in command over Egypt. It turned out that Joseph became the second in command over the entire world!

Let me ask you an honest question—whose plan was better? Joseph's original plan, or God's bigger plan? Joseph learned he was not God, God alone is God, and God is good. God's plans are better than our plans because He is good and always does good things.

**In your own life, where have you wanted control but realized God may have something significantly better for you if you'd just let go?**

I believe one of the most powerful verses in the Bible comes from Joseph's story. As God had planned all along, Joseph's family wound up coming to Egypt, bowing down to Joseph just as he'd seen in his dream, begging for food. After they found out the one they bowed to was Joseph, his brothers realized Joseph had every right to kill them. They panicked and grasped for control of the situation. But Joseph had learned something important about God: He alone is God, and we are not.

> *"Joseph spoke up and told them, 'Don't be afraid. Am I in the place of God? You planned evil against me; God planned it for good to bring about the present result—the survival of many people. Therefore don't be afraid. I will take care of you and your children.' He comforted them and spoke kindly to them."*
> **GENESIS 50:19-21**

Have you experienced God's goodness? If not, maybe God has you exactly where you are, like Zach and Dave, to learn who He is.

**How could God's plan for your life be better than having your dreams or goals come true?**

# [ ON YOUR OWN ]

## DAY 1

## JONAH'S MISSION: I'M NOT GOD

Read Jonah 1. Jonah is a little story about a big God. It's one man's journey, but it describes all of our lives. The primary message of this book is that we are not God.

### Jonah's Plan (Jonah 1:1-3)

The first thing we learn about Jonah is that God had a plan for Jonah's life. God has a plan for all people, including you. He made you, He loves you, and He has a plan for your life. You may be reading this and thinking, "I don't even believe in God," but it doesn't change those facts.

God's plan for Jonah's life involved him going to Nineveh, a city filled with Israel's enemies. Jonah had a plan for his life too—and it didn't involve going to Nineveh. So Jonah ran! We all run from God and say with our choices, "No thanks, my way is better." We resist God's plans for our lives, and even rebel, in countless ways.

When Jonah did his own thing, it didn't work out very well. Look at the passage. How many times do you read the word *down*? That's a tool the writer uses to show us Jonah's trajectory—not up, but down. He was digging a pretty big hole for himself. Notice specifically where he's going. Tarshish isn't just the opposite direction of Nineveh, but on maps available at the time, Tarshish would have been the end of the world. Jonah was trying to get as far away from God as possible. But it's impossible to get away from God. As Jonah would find out—God is everywhere! However, in trying, Jonah got himself into a sticky (literally) situation.

**Could our way ever be better than God's way? Explain.**

## God's Plan (Jonah 1:4-17)

Not all detours are disasters. Learning that we are not God is not always a fun process, but the detours are all designed to point us away from our controlling hands to God's gracious hands. And the detours we experience along the way help us to give up control and trust in God.

**What has God called you to do? Did you obey? What happened?**

Jonah ran away from God's plan and right into some serious detours.

First, God sent a storm. This wasn't just a little rain—it was a raging storm, strong enough to terrify experienced sailors. Then God used the casting of lots to identify Jonah as the guilty party. Jonah might have assumed this was all just a coincidence, but God cleared that up quickly. Since the storm and the casting lots didn't get his attention, God sent a big fish that literally swallowed Jonah alive.

Even though being thrown over the side of a ship in the midst of a crazy storm and being swallowed by a massive fish sound like the worst things imaginable, these detours Jonah experienced weren't disasters at all—they were acts of God's grace. God was helping Jonah understand who is God and who is not. God has a plan for your life. It's bigger, better, and brighter than anything you could ever imagine. Despite the storms you might be experiencing today, despite the detours you've experienced, God is not finished with you. He's teaching you that you aren't God. Are you listening?

**Did you know that God has a plan for your life? What do you think that plan is? How will you respond if you find out it's something else?**

## DAY 2

# JONAH'S MESSAGE: GOD IS GOD

Read Jonah 2. Have you ever been stuck? Stuck in traffic, stuck in a conversation you can't get out of, or maybe stuck in the longest line imaginable? We all get stuck, like when strong winds blew through an amusement park in China and shut down power to one of the park's coasters. This wouldn't have been so bad, except the sixteen thrill-seekers were stuck in the middle of the ride, and left hanging upside-down for half an hour until park workers could get them down.[1] Being stuck stinks.

### Stuck (Jonah 2:1)

Jonah was stuck and it stunk—it literally smelled like fish guts. Three days he sat in the belly of this fish, wallowing in his misery. After all, what else is there to do while stuck inside a fish? A better idea is to pray, and Jonah finally figured that out. Chapter 2 in the Book of Jonah records his prayer. He cried out to God from the lowest possible point. And in that moment, one thing became very clear. Jonah finally acknowledged that God is God.

**When have you been at a low point and cried out to God? What happened?**

Keep in mind what was happening: Jonah had been tossed by the waves, swallowed by a fish, and buried deep in the sea. At that moment, he knew clearly that things were completely out of his control. But Jonah called out to God.

When do you pray the most? If you are like most people, it's when you feel desperate. You likely pray the most when you realize you cannot control something. We need to remember that in our lives and in our pain, just like in Jonah's situation, God is always there. Even though Jonah tried to run away, God was always with him, and Jonah came to understand his own weakness and God's strength.

### Delivered (Jonah 2:2-10)

Jonah said he called (2:2), he cried (2:2), he looked up (2:4), and he remembered (2:7). Since God is God—as He makes very clear—then our calling, crying out, looking up, and remembering Him is not just about our inability, but it's all about His ability. When we hurt, it's often in that moment of pain and questioning that we realize He is God, and He is in control. God did what only He could do for Jonah—He rescued Jonah out of the fish and placed him on dry land and gave Jonah a second chance.

**What do you think it felt like to be stuck inside of the fish for three days?**

God brought Jonah to this place of need to reveal very clearly that He was in control and still had a plan for Jonah's life. This plan involved Jonah's realizing that God alone is God. He alone is in control. Jonah prayed, and he wrote down his prayer for us to read. Jonah's message to everyone throughout history is that we have a great God who is sovereign over our lives.

**When things go wrong in your life, what do you do? Who do you reach out to? After reading this, what do you think you should do differently next time you're stuck?**

**How powerful is prayer? What do you pray for regularly? Why do you think prayer is so important?**

# JONAH'S MIRACLE: GOD IS GOOD

Read Jonah 3 and 4. *Who is God*? Have you ever stepped back to consider that question? If a friend asked you today, "I heard you believe in God, who is He?" how would you respond? Creator, sovereign Lord, heavenly Father, holy—maybe one of the best ways to describe God is—He is good. The psalmist said it this way, "Give thanks to the LORD, for He is good; His faithful love endures forever" (Ps 107:1). If we learn anything from Jonah, it's that God is good.

## God Is Good to His Enemies (Jonah 3)

The whole reason Jonah was sent to Nineveh was to proclaim to people who were far from God: "There's hope!" They weren't only far from God in terms of distance (from Israel and the temple), but they were also far from God spiritually. They were His enemies. They had their own gods, they regularly and brutally attacked Israel, and they lived a lifestyle characterized by terrible sin.

The Bible actually says that *all* sinners are God's enemies. In Romans 5:10, Paul said, "For if, while we were enemies, we were reconciled to God through the death of his Son, then how much more, having been reconciled, will we be saved by his life." The people of Nineveh, as big and bad and proud as they were, were very much like we are today. Apart from God's intervening, we have no hope. Yet, because God is good, He does good things, such as sending a messenger to His enemies. God sent His only Son to die for His enemies—sinners—you and me.

**Describe the feelings that come to mind when you think about being God's enemy.**

We need to remember that God is not taking care of His friends in high places. Rather, He is loving, serving, and giving to those who have rebelled against Him as His enemies. This seems unthinkable! Yet, God does it because He is good.

## God Is Good to His Children (Jonah 4)

God not only loves and reaches out to His enemies, but He also is good to His children. Everyone in Nineveh believed God and they were spared from destruction. They threw a huge party celebrating the mercy and goodness of God—and Jonah hated it! In many ways, Jonah had every right to feel this way. The Assyrians were evil and had killed many of Jonah's (and God's!) own people. Nonetheless, God has chosen to show mercy, and He patiently worked with Jonah through his struggles.

> "We need to remember that God is not taking care of His friends in high places. Rather, He is loving, serving, and giving to those who have rebelled against Him as His enemies."

**When have you been upset because God showed mercy to someone you believed undeserving?**

The last chapter of Jonah's book can be seriously confusing, but don't miss the fact that God continued to be good to Jonah. In many ways, He showed Jonah not just how He cared for Nineveh, but also how He had been good to Jonah every step of the way, caring for him like a son. Despite Jonah's pain, God had a purpose to reveal Himself more clearly and to make Jonah more like Him.

Despite what you feel, do you know that God is good? It may take some work, but look back on your life and I'm sure you will see His kind hands shaping your life. Maybe the place you are at today, like Jonah on the hill, is designed to teach you who God is. God is good and we are called to look back and remember His goodness and to look forward, expecting to "taste and see that the LORD is good" (Ps. 34:8).

**How have you seen God work powerfully in the life of a friend or family member? In your own life?**

**If God could change the whole city of Nineveh just through Jonah's few words, what could God do through your life? Why do we sometimes assume God doesn't want to use us to do important things?**

Have you ever asked God to use you? Have you ever prayed a big dream that only God could do through you? Take a few minutes and ask God what He could do through your life that only He could do if you were willing to obey Him no matter the risk. Write it down. Pray over it and ask God to give you confirmation and encouragement to follow Him, even if it takes you into the belly of a big fish!

# BROKEN

PSALM 51:4

## WATCH

In this scene, Zach meets Ginger's family for the first time. It's exactly what you would think the first dinner with someone's parents would be like—tense. The heart of this scene is when Mr. Grayson asks Zach what he thinks about Jesus. Some conversations are difficult, but they are necessary. Zach may never have thought about it until that moment, but he had a broken relationship with God, and it became painfully obvious as he and Ginger parted that evening.

## DISCUSS

**Why did Zach struggle with Jesus? Who do you resonate with more—Zach or Ginger?**

The biggest problem in our lives is our broken relationship with God. We may experience a lot of difficulties, and we may find ourselves in some tough places, but the root of all our problems is sin. It sometimes takes an honest conversation to help us see that our relationship with God is broken.

**When has an honest conversation helped you rethink the way you were living?**

When the Titanic was built, it was the largest moving man-made structure in the world, and many saw it as a floating miracle. The ship cost $7.5 million in 1912, which would be the equivalent of almost $190 million today.[1] As you know though, the ship many called "unsinkable" was certainly sinkable. In the early morning hours of April 15, 1912, the large cruise liner collided with an iceberg, and the size of the ship was nothing compared to the massive chunk of ice.

The majority of an iceberg, as much as 90 percent in fact, is hidden underwater. This same principle can be observed every day in your kitchen. The next time you have a glass of ice water, notice how much of the ice sits below the surface. Due to the density of ice compared to water, what is completely unseen underneath the surface is significantly bigger and more important than the things we see. This had huge consequences for the Titanic, and what is below the surface matters just as much in our lives today.

**What are some things that hold you back from trusting Christ?**

**What does it mean that sin is the root issue behind all our problems?**

The scene where Zach has dinner with the Graysons is one of the most important scenes in the whole movie. It's important because it reveals underlying issues—the things in Zach's heart. To this point in the movie, we haven't clearly understood where Zach stands with God. He could quote Bible verses to Ginger in the hospital, but at the same time, he avoided going to church with Dave. This scene is crucial because it is the first time we see Zach coming face-to-face with his ideas about Jesus—looking beneath the surface and deeper into his own heart. Some conversations are vital not because of what's said, but because of what's revealed.

In 2005, the television network A&E launched a new show called *Intervention*. The premise of the show was to follow an individual who had a problem, whether they knew it or not, through a confrontation or "intervention," and then hopefully through rehabilitation. It was such a popular show that in 2009 it won an Emmy for "Outstanding Reality Program."[2] It was often heartbreaking because it showcased the power of addiction and the destruction experienced by whole families because of one person's choices. What was even more alarming was that people were actually surprised at their interventions.

Have you ever had an honest conversation in which someone challenged you, and you realized something was wrong? To the point that it was beyond your ability to fix it? Have you ever been confronted by someone you loved? In 2 Samuel 11 and 12, we are given a glimpse into King David's life, including his sin, and through his conversation with Nathan, we can see the state of David's broken heart. It's an Old Testament intervention.

## A Broken Life (2 Sam. 11)

David was the king. He started at the bottom and rose to the top of the nation of Israel. He was the youngest son of Jesse, and he wasn't particularly impressive (1 Sam. 16). He was a shepherd boy who spent his time with the animals, but one day God called on him to face a giant. In fact, God called David to face two giants! After he killed Goliath, he had to live with Saul, Israel's giant. David became very popular among the people, and Saul was jealous—so jealous that he tried again and again to kill David.

After Saul was killed in battle and David assumed the throne, he did some amazing and kingly things. However, beneath the surface was a broken heart, which we glimpse in 2 Samuel 11. The passage opens with statements that are at least a little confusing. It was the time when kings went to war, and while Israel was engaged in battle in Rabbah, David remained in Jerusalem. Further, it was night time, but David was wide awake. He should have been in bed, but David was somewhere else. This is all a description of how backward life was for David. His heart was out of line, and his actions followed his heart.

**When has your heart been "out of line"? How did your actions follow your heart?**

David did something completely wicked. The one God described as "a man after His own heart," chose to forsake God, violate the wife of one of his soldiers, and threaten the whole nation of Israel with his carelessness and sin. David though because he had worked to cover up his sins that he could just move on. The problem is, we cannot get away with sin. It always has a consequence and a cost. Very soon, Bathsheba came to David with the news that their sin had consequences. Bathsheba was pregnant! David had a choice, and he made maybe the worst choice possible. Instead of owning up to his sin and accepting the consequences, he chose to cover it up at any cost. His plan involved the murder of Bathsheba's husband, Uriah.

If we don't study the Old Testament carefully we can miss that Bathsheba's father and husband, Eliam and Uriah, were part of a group called "mighty men" who served King David (2 Sam. 23). These were an elite group of warriors who lived with David and fought for him. They took great risks and accomplished heroic feats. For instance, Josheb-basshebeth killed 800 men in one battle using only a spear (2 Sam. 23:8). God used them in mighty ways to accomplish His purposes in David's life, but in desperation to cover up his sin, David was willing to kill one of them. Though David didn't physically carry out the murder, he was no less responsible before God.

How does something like this happen? David, the giant killer and the people's champion, the one who refused to kill Saul, even when all others thought he had the right, had become an adulterer and murderer. Have you ever been surprised at the things you've done? Maybe more surprising is the ways we try to justify those things.

**What are some ways you've tried to justify actions that were clearly wrong?**

The chapter ends as wildly as it begins. Uriah was out of the picture, Bathsheba became his bride, and David thought he'd solved all his problems. Yet "the LORD considered what David had done to be evil" (2 Sam. 11:27). We all do things that make no sense—even in our own minds—things we wish no one would ever know about. We're all broken.

## A Conversation about Brokenness (2 Sam. 12)

Nathan was David's friend. He was also God's prophet. A prophet was a spokesman for God—a person called to give a specific message from God to His people. God sent Nathan to speak to David about his broken life, heart, and situation. Nathan and David, like Ginger and Zach, had an honest conversation about their hearts. Nathan began with a powerful story, and David was astounded. "Who is this man who stole the sheep?" As readers, it may be difficult for us to understand his confusion and anger, but David thought he had taken care of his problems. We all do. We all think we can manage our sin. But, even when we think we have our sin under control, sin is more destructive than we can ever imagine. It's the opposite of controllable—it's dominating.

No one likes being confronted. Yet, confrontations can save our lives. Jerrell Freeman was a linebacker for the Chicago Bears. When he was on his way to spring training in July 2017, he stopped for BBQ in the Austin airport. While he was eating, he noticed another man in the restaurant acting oddly, frantically moving around the restaurant. Jerrell realized the man was choking on his brisket, so he jumped up, grabbed the man, and hit two times him on his back. The man, shaken but relieved, looked up and said to Jerrell, "I think you just saved my life!"[3]

When he recognized the issue, Jerrell knew he had to do something. That's exactly what Nathan did—he confronted David because he knew that lives were on the line if he didn't. Nathan pointed the finger at David, who was angered by the story, and said to him, "You are the man!" (2 Sam. 12:7). This wasn't just a story to entertain David, it was meant to hit him where it hurts—in the heart.

**Describe a time when someone's confrontation hit you in the heart. What changes in your life, if any, resulted from this conversation?**

How would you feel if someone knew everything you ever did? They knew what you ate for dinner last Thursday, who your third-grade teacher was, or about the time you lied to your parents about the reason you were home late. They know *everything*! Would that freak you out? Here's the thing—God *does* know everything. He's with you, everywhere, all the time. Nathan could speak to David's sin, not because he was especially perceptive, super smart, or a psychic, but because he'd received a message from God. According to what God revealed to him, Nathan spelled out David's sin, point by painful point.

Imagine how that felt. If you stood right now in front of God, the holy and righteous judge, what would you say? It can be easy to think we can manage our sin, but it's just not possible, and one day we will stand before God to account for every thought and action. Further, His standard isn't good and bad as we see it—it's holy—moral perfection. According to that standard, we're all guilty. And as David learned, no one can hide their sins.

**Have you ever had an honest conversation with someone about what you really think about God? What did you say?**

> "God confronts us because He loves us. When we confess, God brings restoration to our brokenness."

## A Broken Relationship with God (Ps. 51)

The most important question we can answer is this: What do we do with our sin?

Simply put, sin is breaking God's rules. Therefore, if we don't have clearly defined rules, or if we change and redefine the rules we do have, we can find ways to feel okay about our lives. However, in working to manage or suppress sin in this way is foolish. We may be "not guilty" in a worldly sense, but this only adds to our guilt before God.

The only way to deal with our sin is to confess it. This may seem like the last thing we'd want to do—after all, once we confess it, we own it. But to be made right with God, we have to be honest about our condition both with ourselves and with Him. Confession isn't about managing sin; it's about agreeing that we are guilty. It's about admitting our inability to control sin and our need for Him. God confronts us because He loves us. When we confess, God brings restoration to our brokenness.

**Why do you think it's so difficult to admit to God we've done wrong? Explain.**

Psalm 51 is David's confession. He begins by focusing on the fact that God is God, and he is not. David says in verse four, "Against you—you alone—I have sinned and done this evil in your sight." (Ps. 51:4) This may seem odd. After all, Bathsheba had become pregnant, and Uriah was dead. And there were many more people David's sin affected. Since God created all things, including us, and has ordered all things according to His purposes, while we may impact and inflict others with our sins, all sin is breaking His rules and order and is therefore against Him primarily. David recognized that his sin was horrible, and he said in essence, "God, I'm aware of my sin, it's terrible, and it's all been against You!"

Since our sin is primarily against God, it's initial consequence is that it separates us from God. Though David's sin hurt many, he recognized that ultimately he had broken God's rules and God's heart. Because of his offense, his relationship with God was shattered. All other issues seemed small compared with the weight of this reality. He finally did the right thing and cried out to God for grace and mercy.

All of us are broken because of our sin. Further, our relationship with God is broken because of our sin. But God graciously sends people like Nathan to confront us. This study may be that conversation for you. Have you recognized the ways you've offended God and confessed? Zach had to admit he didn't have the same kind of relationship with Jesus Ginger or her parents did. But things didn't have to stay that way, and the same is true for you. God is gracious and merciful. If you confess, He will forgive you and restore you.

**Describe a time you confessed to God how much you need Him. What brought you to that point?**

**What specifically do you need to confess and who will you talk with about it?**

# [ ON YOUR OWN ]

## THE RUN-AWAY

In Luke 15, we read three stories of lost things: a lost sheep, a lost coin, and a lost son. A crowd of tax collectors and sinners had gathered to hear Jesus teach, and the Pharisees and scribes were there as well—complaining. It's possible they were criticizing Jesus for spending time with the outcasts of society. However, they were more likely complaining that crowds were coming to Jesus for wisdom instead of to them, the established religious leaders. Jesus used the opportunity to address both groups, the "sinners" and the "righteous." He took the opportunity to teach parables that pointed to the true gospel.

### A Lost Heart (Luke 15:11-13)

When Jesus looked at the crowd, He saw two types of people. There were "sinners"—those society saw as broken, foolish, defiled, and enemies of God who needed to get their act together. There were also the Pharisees—those who were "righteous." They did all the right things, and everyone knew it. With these distinctly different kinds of people in His presence, having already shared two brief stories, Jesus continued with the third parable of lost things. But this time it wasn't a sheep, coin, or some other object; it was a child.

The story begins with a scandal. The younger son said to his father, "I want my inheritance right now," because he didn't care to be under the authority of his father any longer. He wanted to be independent, but he couldn't do it on his own—he "depended" on his father for this. See the irony? Before he even left home, his heart was long gone. So when the father gave him the inheritance, he took the money and ran.

> **When have you gotten something you wanted but realized it wasn't what you wanted at all?**

### A Lost Life (Luke 15:14-20)

*Prodigal* is a term that may not be familiar to many of us. The word means *reckless* or *wasteful*, especially regarding money or lifestyle. This young man lost his way and had been lost by his family, and this was expressed in his lifestyle and spending. Soon enough, he foolishly wasted all his father had given him. He wound up broke and in desperate poverty because the country where he'd moved fell into famine. Things were bad. To make things worse, the only work that he could find in this far away land was to feed pigs. This may not seem that bad to you but to a Jew, pigs were unclean. It would have meant further separation from everything he knew. In his desperation, he longed to eat the pig's food because he had nothing. He was hopeless. He was lost. He was the perfect picture of a sinner.

**In what ways are you running from God?**

As Jesus taught, the sinners were listening intently. Their hearts were diseased, they had made disastrous decisions, they had hurt others by their rebellious living, and they had lived wastefully in many ways. These sinners were bad people—just like everybody else! The truth is, apart from God's intervening grace, all people are sinners. We all want to take God's blessings, and then run away to do things our own way. But the things we run to—things we think will make us feel important, define us, or solve all our problems— always lead us to the same place as the prodigal son. We become desperate and hopeless. But the good news of the gospel is that God loves broken sinners so much that He sent His only Son to rescue them from their lostness.

**How are we all hopeless apart from God's intervention?**

**What do you think the "sinners" in the crowd heard Jesus saying to them?**

# DAY 2

## LOST BROTHER (RUNNING AWAY AT HOME)

### Working for Love (Luke 15:25-30)

In the story we often call "The Prodigal Son," there are actually two sons. In fact, Jesus even began with, "A man had two sons" (Luke 15:11). One son didn't care to live under his father's love and authority: He ran far away, did scandalous things, and found himself absolutely lost. While one son was running, the other son was working. But he didn't do it for the right reasons. When his father held a feast to celebrate the younger brother's returning home, the older brother basically threw a tantrum and refused to participate. He complained, "Look, I have been slaving many years for you, and I have never disobeyed your orders, yet you never gave me a goat so that I could celebrate with my friends" (Luke 15:29). He had obeyed his father, but out of obligation, seeking what the father could give him—not from love and devotion. He'd kept all the rules, but he was really no closer to his father than the younger brother.

**Why do you think we're often tempted to believe that keeping the rules is more important than our motives for doing so?**

Have you ever considered that it can be just as dangerous to keep all the rules as it is to break them? The Pharisees who heard this story were known to do and say all the right things, but they were no closer to God than the tax collectors and sinners. They were lost.

When people consider standing before God and His asking them, "Why should I let you into heaven?" many would say, "Because I have been a good person." We can all think of someone who is worse than us. So we get the false sense that God is pleased because we may be "better" than others. The problem is that the Bible never says, "be good" or "be better." God's standard isn't good—it's holy. You can avoid cursing, drinking, rated R movies, or any other sinful behaviors, but still be lost.

Tim Keller said it this way, "Neither son loved the father for himself. They both were using the father for their own self-centered ends rather than loving, enjoying, and serving him for his own sake. This means that you can rebel against God and be alienated from him either by breaking his rules or by keeping all of them diligently. It's a shocking message: Careful obedience to God's law may serve as a strategy for rebelling against God."[4]

## Love Worked for Us (Luke 15:31-32)

Jesus told the Pharisees it's impossible to be "good enough." God isn't after your actions—He's after your heart. We often avoid God by working hard and doing the right things, but it won't work. Working hard to keep the rules makes us no less a prodigal than if we broke them all. Our need is much greater than we're able to repair by being good. Thankfully, God gives grace to those who turn to Him. Jesus came to accomplish by His works what we couldn't by ours. Trust in Jesus and rest in what He has done.

**Can we be good enough for God? Why or why not?**

**Rebellion and sin can be in our actions or our attitudes, but they originate from the heart. Are you more like the older brother or the younger brother?**

**How specifically can you grow in your love for God?**

**What do you think the Pharisees thought when they heard this?**

## LOVING FATHER (HE RUNS FOR US)

Jesus spoke to both the Pharisees and the sinners in the crowd. He wanted them to know that they were all on equal ground—far away from God and hopelessly lost. But God's grace could change all that, and the real focal point of the parable is not the sons, but the father.

### The Fatherly God (Luke 15:20-22)

God designed it that all dads would be kind and loving, but not all dads do this well. Tragically, many kids grow up without a dad in their lives, and maybe the worst part is that earthly fathers are meant to be clear representations of God. He wants all people to see Him as our heavenly Father. Because no dad is perfect, you may have to look beyond your father to see this, but God is a good Father, in the fullest sense.

**How does it affect your perception of God to know that He is an even better Father than the one described in this parable?**

The father Jesus describes in the parable is a good father. He is not selfish. He is not concerned about his image. He is not angry. This father is a picture of the love all fathers are supposed to have for their children.

## The Prodigal God (Luke 15:23-24)

The father's love was a bit prodigal if you think about it. He lavishly gave it away. God, our heavenly Father, gave His Son freely for us. Jesus gave His life for ours. Why? Because He loves us. Your broken heart will never find restoration until you look up and see God running for you. His hands are outstretched to embrace you, but it starts with that realization of our inability and need for help.

**Does this picture influence the way you see God's love? Why or why not?**

Remember the definition of *prodigal*: reckless or wasteful. One more idea defines the word: to spend until there's nothing left. In the parable, the father was recklessly generous, refusing to hold the son's sins against him, instead lavishly celebrating his return. Our heavenly Father's love is like that. The sacrifice He gave on our behalf was far greater than we'll ever appreciate. In fact, Jesus emptied Himself—giving even His life— so we could be brought home to God.

The master painter Rembrandt regularly painted himself into his paintings, and experts estimate that he has over 40 self-portraits, including his painting "The Raising of the Cross." In this masterpiece, he is clearly seen at the foot of the cross helping to crucify Jesus. Rembrandt also painted the story of the prodigal son, and chose out of all the characters to paint himself as the father. Rembrandt's life was tragically marked by suffering. By the time he completed this painting, he had endured the death of his wife, three children, and two ladies who had lived him within his home. He knew what it felt like to experience the loss of a child. He longed to be the father who could embrace the son who returned home.[5] God loves us this way. He's not waiting for us to clean up our act, to get it right, and stop sinning.

Our lives and hearts are broken beyond repair, but God is a miracle-working God who runs to His children and restores them with His love. He throws the biggest party to celebrate our return, and He loves us lavishly. He is the prodigal God.

**What do you think about when you think about God?**

**How has God run after you? Why do you think Jesus references a party after the lost are found?**

# [ FORGIVENESS— THE STARTING LINE ]

EPHESIANS 1:7-10

# WATCH

While Nanny and Dave await the results of Zach's surgery, they have an important conversation. Michael, Dave and Zach's father, not only abandoned them after their mother's death, but has sinned against them in numerous ways since. The boys have a broken relationship with their father, and it's only gotten worse. Nanny encourages Dave to forgive his dad, not because his dad deserves it or has given any sign of change, but because forgiveness is the start.

Fast forward to the cemetery. This is the first time that Michael has seen Zach and Dave in awhile. Again, Michael is in no position to be forgiven, and Zach responds as he always has—in anger. However, Dave decides to write a new story and forgives his dad. We have no clue what can happen after we forgive those who have hurt us. Forgiveness is the start, and forgiveness can change everything.

# DISCUSS

**What did Nanny mean by, "We'd be surprised how much can change when we start to forgive others"?**

In 1995, park rangers at Yellowstone National Park released fourteen gray wolves into the park. Wolves in that region had been heavily hunted from the late 1800s into the early 1900s until the gray wolf population in that region was decimated. The release would mark the first time the gray wolf roamed that terrain since 1920. With no natural predator in that region, the deer and elk populations had grown out of control, and as the wolves spread out, the first sign of their presence was the thinning out of the deer and elk. As these decreased, berry producing plants and trees that were primary food sources for the deer and elk began to return. This brought back rodents to the region and with the rodents came mid-sized predators like foxes, hawks, and bald eagles. With the regrowth of the trees came beaver, which affected the rivers in the park, which also brought back specific fish species that had not been in the park for decades. Here's the point: fourteen wolves changed the entire ecosystem of Yellowstone National Park.[1] If wolves can change an ecosystem, think of what can God do in your life.

**Why is it so difficult to forgive? Why is it so difficult to ask to be forgiven?**

# FORGIVENESS IS THE STARTING LINE

We rarely think about the power of small beginnings. It's ingrained in us, in a sense, to focus on outcomes and not necessarily on when and where and how something begins. Think about an avalanche. National Geographic says, "Avalanches are most common in the 24 hours directly following a storm that dumps 12 inches or more of fresh snow. The quick pileup overloads the underlying snowpack, which causes a weak layer beneath the slab to fracture."[2] Here's the crazy thing—the violence and power of a natural avalanche, one not caused by a skier or snowmobile, all starts with one snowflake. When that last flake lands and tips the scale of how much weight can be supported, it launches an avalanche. Hurricanes start small, too. The strongest storms to hit the United States— the ones with over 157 mile-per-hour winds—all start as a breeze in the Sahara.[3]

Nanny looked Dave in the eyes and challenged him to see the potential, not the current reality. Michael was guilty: He had abandoned his boys and had become an alcoholic who took advantage of people to get what he wanted. However, Nanny wasn't looking at the problem; she saw the potential. One snowflake and a simple breeze may look insignificant, but they are the beginnings of something huge.

**Why do you think it's often easier to look at the problem rather than the potential?**

Just like Zach and Dave, sometimes the pain in our past can be so daunting that we cannot see past it. Sometimes the wounds are so deep that we cannot feel anything else. Nanny understood this, and she knew things were unlikely to change if the boys couldn't move beyond the pain. "Maybe he doesn't know how… Maybe he's too proud… Maybe he's too broken." Michael was all those things, but the situation doesn't determine the outcome, God does. "You'd be surprised how things can start to change when you forgive someone," was Nanny's way of saying, one snowflake can start an avalanche.

Paul's assessment of the Ephesian believers' past was bleak at best.

> *You were dead in your trespasses and sins. … You were without Christ,*
> *excluded from the citizenship of Israel, and foreigners to the covenants*
> *of promise, without hope and without God in the world.*
> **EPHESIANS 2:1,12**

Those are big statements! We are dead and without hope without God. I don't know of any situation that could be worse. That's the background for the gospel truth Paul drops on the church in Ephesians 1:7-10. Paul tells us God initiates forgiveness, and forgiveness changes everything!

## Jesus Was Sinned Against (Eph. 1:7)

We've looked at the fact that God is God and we are not. But Paul mentions our trespasses here. He is in control, yet we all step in and try to take the reins. We've also seen that we're all broken. We do and think the wrong things, but Paul says we are spiritually dead. Though our sin hurts many others, it's primarily against God (Ps. 51). To truly appreciate what Jesus has done for us, we need to start with the truth about ourselves.

**In your own words, describe the truth about humanity according to this verse.**

No conversation about forgiveness should start without honesty. We've all sinned against God, and if we want to consider forgiving someone else, it starts with being honest about the fact that they sinned against you. It could be something as simple as being lied to or as complicated as being abused or abandoned. The Bible never downplays your pain or asks you to ignore it. God doesn't ignore our sin or place it out of sight—He deals with it. Because we've been wronged, forgiveness can be tough, but it allows us to experience something significantly greater than our hurts.

> "The gospel isn't the good news of what we can do for ourselves, but of what has been done by Jesus."

## Jesus Initiates Forgiveness (Eph. 1:7-8)

Paul explains that our redemption comes through Jesus' blood; it's all because of Him. Jesus initiates our forgiveness. He went to a cross and died in our place, was resurrected in our place, and ascended in our place before any of us were born. The gospel isn't the good news of what we can do for ourselves, but of what has been done by Jesus.

If you aren't a Christian and you're reading this: This is for you! Jesus initiated the forgiving process. He didn't wait for us to confess or change, but chose to sacrifice Himself while we were still sinners.

**Why does God initiate forgiveness?**

**How is this different from the way you tend to think about your salvation?**

## Jesus Paid to Forgive Us (Eph. 1:7-8)

Have you ever heard someone say: "If it was easy, everyone would do it"? Forgiveness is *not* easy. It's looking into the eyes of the person who has hurt you and telling them you're letting the pain go. It costs us something to forgive, but this price must be paid for reconciliation to occur. It cost Jesus His life for us to have a relationship with God. It cost God His only Son.

Up until that moment, for all eternity past the Trinity had existed in perfect love, perfect relationship, and perfect community. As Jesus took our sins on Himself, the greatest pain wasn't the nails or the crown of thorns, but being separated from the Father. John Stott said, "Divine love triumphed over divine wrath by divine self-sacrifice."[4] Jesus paid the penalty for our sins—He was beaten, crucified, pierced, and separated from the Father. Paul calls these actions on our behalf "riches" of His grace, which are "richly" poured out. In the Greek it says His forgiveness occurs through His wealth, which He has caused to overflow toward us. There is literally nothing more valuable than Jesus, and God has poured Him out for us. In the words of the old hymn, "Jesus paid it all."

**When you think about the pain it caused both God and Jesus to forgive our sins, how does that affect your willingness to forgive others?**

## Jesus' Forgiveness Produces Change (Eph. 1:7-10)

Redemption comes through forgiveness, and forgiveness produces freedom. The word *redemption* means ransom. Paul is essentially saying Jesus paid our debt, and His payment—His act of forgiving us—secures our freedom. But Paul's emphasis shifts from the past to the future. God has a plan for our lives, and it pleased Him to send Jesus to take our place, because His plan is to reunite His family.

God is on a mission to rescue His children, but that's not all. God is also doing an amazing work in and through us. God has forgiven us so we would join Him in His work. We went from being an enemy to being a child, from being dead to alive, from being absorbed in ourselves to commissioned to join God in His global work.

It's a small moment—maybe a conversation, a letter, an email, a text, whatever—that marks the road to forgiveness. The first drop of rain initiates the downpour. Forgiveness doesn't mean we downplay the wrong; instead we initiate the right. There is a cost, but it may be the down payment on something unimaginable. We have no clue what God can do when we follow His lead and forgive our enemies. When we ask for God's forgiveness, we can't begin to imagine how it changes our story.

**How has God's act of forgiveness changed your story? How might your forgiveness introduce someone else to His?**

In May of 2002, Ike woke up to a knock at his door. Ike was a police officer, and when he opened the door, his Chief, Sergeant, Lieutenant, and the Chaplain of his police department were standing there. Ike was confused until his Sergeant said, "Ike, I've got to tell you that your son was killed." Ike said Issac was, "a good kid." He had been at a friend's house that night playing video games when Takoya Criner shot and killed both Isaac and his friend, Jeffrey. It would be three years before the court case, and Ike didn't know what he would do or what he would say when he saw his son's killer. When the day came for the trial, Ike said, "I got there, and I saw him for the first time, and I loved him. I didn't know him. I had never seen him before, and yet I loved him."

Ike began to write letters to Takoya, but could never bring himself to mail them. One day, he wrote a letter that said, "I miss my son, will you fill in for him? I'd love to come see you in prison." This letter he actually mailed. Meanwhile, Takoya had been dealing with the weight of his actions. He asked God to forgive him but struggled to forgive himself. He prayed, "God, if I hear from Mr. Brown, I will know you're real and I will give you the rest of my life." That day, he received the letter that Mr. Brown had sent including his request to come see him. Takoya agreed to meet. When the guards opened the doors, Mr. Brown ran in and bear-hugged Takoya. Ike couldn't bring his son back, but he could forgive his son's killer. When he forgave, it changed everything. In a sense, Mr. Brown got a new son, and Takoya got a new father. Forgiveness changed the story."[5]

This story is an illustration of what God has done for us. God has forgiven those responsible for the death of His son. Further, He's adopted us as His own sons and daughters, and He has changed our eternity. Have you been forgiven? It's the starting point, the first snowflake. And it's the beginning of something much bigger than we could ever imagine.

**How does an understanding of how much you've been forgiven compel you to forgive others?**

**How do you initiate forgiveness?**

# [ ON YOUR OWN ]

## DAY 1

### YOU'VE BEEN FORGIVEN MUCH

#### The Debt (Matt. 18:21-35)

Visualize the parable. A king decided to collect all the debts his people owed him. One servant owed him what might as well have been an infinite debt—it was absolutely impossible to pay! So the king ordered the servant, as well as his family, to be sold so a portion of the debt could be paid. The servant begged the king, "Please have patience. I'll pay everything, I promise!" But the king, a kind and generous leader, had compassion and forgave the entire debt. No payment plans, no working off the debt—just straight-up forgiveness.

What happens next is mind blowing. Another man owed the servant an insignificant amount of money, especially compared to the debt he had owed the king. The variance in numbers is meant to catch our attention because it was chump change in comparison. Yet, as soon as the servant leaves the king's palace, he tracks down the man who owned him and begins to choke him screaming, "Pay what you owe!" When the man couldn't pay his minor debt, the servant had him thrown in jail. The king heard this outrageous story and called for the servant to return to the palace. He had the wicked servant thrown in jail because he refused to forgive after he'd been forgiven.

> **Why do you think Jesus used the analogy of debt in this parable? How does this help you understand what Christ has done for you?**

Here's Jesus' point. In His kingdom, forgiveness has no limits because He has forgiven us of more sin than we could ever calculate.

## The Forgiven (Matt. 18:21-35)

Treason is the act of making war against your home country. This also includes giving aid or comfort to enemies, or aligning with the enemy in any manner. In the United States, treason is a crime punishable by death. But think about this: Sin is also treason, because anytime we forsake God's way, we are betraying Him and aligning with the kingdom of darkness.

**Have you ever thought of your sin as an act of treason? How will this view change the way you live?**

The Bible says we are all debtors. Because we owe so much to God, we are in an impossible situation. When we realize how badly we've sinned against God—how it's added up over the years and been multiplied by interest—we should realize our spiritual bankruptcy and beg God for forgiveness. Think about all the ways you've sinned—ignored God, broken His rules, loved other things more than Him, missed the perfect mark of holiness—and the amount of debt that has accumulated against you. For every one of us, it's an infinite debt, and we all deserve the punishment of death and hell.

God can't simply ignore our sins. God doesn't avoid our sins—and even forgiveness has certain requirements. If a guilty criminal stood before a judge who avoided dealing with the facts, ignored the facts, or just dismissed them, then that judge would not be just. But God is just. He required payment for our forgiveness, and Jesus paid our debt with His life. Here's what's even crazier; we're not talking about past debt only, but Jesus has paid for all the sin we will ever commit—past, present, and future. The debt for sin was impossibly great, but Jesus paid it by giving His life for ours.

**What are appropriate responses to being forgiven a debt this size? How should we live in light of what Christ has done for us?**

# FORGIVEN PEOPLE FORGIVE

## Forgiven People (Matt. 18:21-35)

Can you imagine winning the lottery? On Wednesday, August 23, 2017, Mavis Wanczyk won the largest single lottery ticket jackpot in U.S. History. She won the Powerball lottery, which had a $758.7 million jackpot. After fees and taxes, Mavis took home $480 million.[6] Can you imagine Mavis receiving that check on Wednesday, then on Thursday heading to her old job demanding the $50 a co-worker owed her? That would be insane, right?! That's Jesus' point. For those who've received forgiveness for sin, it makes even less sense to withhold forgiveness from others.

**When have you withheld forgiveness from someone? How does this truth encourage you to forgive now? Explain.**

## Forgive People (Col. 3:12-13)

In Colossians 3, Paul shares about what life looks like for Christians. As those who have been adopted and received unbelievable love, we are now encouraged to pour out what has been poured into us. We are to forbear and to forgive because we have been forgiven.

Forbearing means to overlook minor offenses. The offense can be as simple as someone cutting you off in traffic or accidentally bumping into you in the hall. We are called to let go of the little things. But some things are difficult, even impossible, to overlook. We are still called to forgive. Here's the tough part: There are no conditions or exceptions. It doesn't say to forgive "unless"; Jesus didn't include any exceptions. Forgiven people are called to forgive. Period.

**What offenses do you find most difficult to forgive? Why?**

We may wonder what forgiveness looks like, but our forgiveness should be a lot like God's forgiveness toward us. We don't ignore the wrong, but we deal with it. It's okay to go to others and let them know about the pain they caused. You can be specific and direct without injuring others. The point is never to make the other person pay, but to bring restoration to the relationship.

A few years ago, an opinion poll asked what phrases people most want to hear. The top three responses were, "I love you," "I forgive you," and "Dinner's ready."[7] The words "I forgive you" may be some of the most powerful words you'll ever speak. When we forgive, we release the other person from debt and guilt. As difficult as this may be, we can never come close to forgiving as much as God has forgiven us. God serves as the perfect example, and we have an endless supply of grace and forgiveness we can tap into. Let's share it generously.

**Why do you think it is so hard to forgive those who have wronged or hurt us?**

## FORGIVENESS CHANGES EVERYTHING

God doesn't ignore our sins, avoid them, or merely let them go. God doesn't act like our sins are any more or less than what they actually are, but He deals with them. This means there was a price for sin. Although we deserve death and hell, Jesus stepped in and took our punishment on Himself. In order to understand what this really means, let's consider our verses from today's personal study.

### Our sins are removed (Ps. 103:12)

Our sins are completely removed. The phrase "east to west" literally means God puts infinite space between us and our sin. God has separated us from our sins as far as either direction—east or west—extends. (Hint: They go on infinitely.) Even when you think about the worst thing you've done, you can rest in the truth that God has erased that sin.

**How is this infinite distance between you and your sins comforting? Take a minute to write out or speak aloud a prayer of praise for what God has forgiven you for.**

### Our sins are no longer remembered (Isa. 43:25)

God will not remember your sins because He chooses not to recall them. He has decided never to bring up everything you've ever done or ever will do. He will hold none of your sins against you. When we're forgiven, God refuses any longer to hold our sins against us. He doesn't simply forgive and forget—after all, God knows everything. Rather, He actively chooses never to bring our sins up again, and treats us as if they never happened.

**What does God's response to our sin teach us about the way we should respond when others sin against us?**

## Our sins are covered (Ps. 32:1-2)

God blesses us by covering our sins. When the prodigal son came home, the father ran to meet him and wrapped him in his nicest robe—he covered his son's filth and nakedness (Luke 15). This is a picture of what God has done for us. When God sees us, He doesn't see our filth, He sees Christ's righteousness. When we look honestly at ourselves, we may not like what we see. But for those who are in Christ, God sees His righteousness when He looks at us.

**Why should this truth change the way you view God's love for you? Your view of who you are? Explain.**

## Our sins are cast into the depths of the ocean (Mic. 7:18-19)

For children of God, this is what God has done with our sin. However, many of us go through life without giving much thought to the implications of the gospel. Receiving God's forgiveness changes everything. We are not who we once were. We're not simply a product of the choices we've made in the past. We are forgiven! This means we are free to do some radical things—like forgive those who hurt us and love even those who hate us. We can do these things because it's what God has done for us. It's amazing to know our past is taken care of, our future is secured, and our identity is found in Jesus. Forgiveness changes everything, including you.

**Which of the truths about God's forgiveness stands out to you? Why?**

**What freedoms does forgiveness—of both past and future sins—bring?**

# TRANSFORMING LOVE

ROMANS 5:6-11

## WATCH

In this scene, Zach is afraid because Dave's latest seizure is worse than anything he's seen before. When he steps out of the room and sees Nanny, it's not that he is upset with her— it's just that everything God has been doing in his life comes to a head at this moment. He blows up at Nanny, who can relate to the way Zach is feeling. She sits down and shares the story of her struggles, but also how, through it all, God always demonstrated His love.

## DISCUSS

**As Nanny looks back on her life, how can she see God's love?**

**How would you define love, in your own words?**

This is one of the biggest ideas in the world—God loves you! The God who created the celestial night sky, who handcrafted Mt. Everest and the Mariana Trench, who designed the vast brilliant colors we see in plant and animal life in our world—this great God says, "I love you." The big idea is this: No matter who you are, what you've done, and what you will do, you are loved by God.

**Why is it sometimes difficult to believe God loves us?**

**What difference does a love like this make in our lives?**

Kurt was born in Burlington, Iowa, and he was a good kid and a decent athlete. He ended up getting a college scholarship to the University of Northern Iowa where he never made it beyond being the third quarterback on their roster for three years. However, during his senior year, Kurt earned the starting role and became the Gateway Conference's Offensive Play of the Year. Kurt ended up going undrafted, as expected, and figured football was over—that is, until he got a call from the Green Bay Packers. He was invited to training camp. Though living up to the likes of Brett Favre and Mark Brunell was unlikely, it was a chance, and Kurt had high hopes.

> "No matter who you are, what you've done, and what you will do, you are loved by God."

But those hopes were dashed when the Packers didn't work out, so Kurt took a job making $5.50 an hour stocking shelves at a local grocery store. Though depressed and confused, Kurt knew God had a plan. He learned during this time about how much God loved him. Soon, Kurt found another job coaching at his old college and continued to grow in his faith, and to train. He eventually got a call from the Iowa Barnstormers, an arena league football team. His hard work and dedication paid off as he led his team to two arena bowls in a row. As Kurt continued to improve, he earned spots in a European football league where he experienced great success.

Then, it happened! Kurt earned a spot playing quarterback for the St. Louis Rams. But he was still third string. Kurt continued to pray, trust God, and work hard. Through a series of trades in 1999, Kurt moved up to second on the depth chart. And after the starter was injured in the preseason, the Rams found themselves with an unknown starting at quarterback. Kurt Warner would go on to be a part of the "Greatest Show on Turf," with three consecutive 500-point seasons. Kurt played in three Super Bowls, winning Super Bowl XXXIV and receiving Super Bowl MVP honors.[1]

Kurt's story is similar to Nanny's—one of pain and difficulty and of learning that God is always present and working. Though we can't always see it at the time, God's way always works out significantly better than we would ever imagine.

**Take a minute to think about the pain and difficulty you've experienced—maybe you're even hurting right now. How has God worked through those situations in your life?**

## GOD LOVES US LIKE CRAZY

Dwight L. Moody—famous pastor and founder of Chicago's Moody Bible Church—traveled to England from 1881-1884 on his second missionary trip. Through one of his campaigns at Cambridge University, the Lord called seven young men to take the gospel to China. These seven would later be named the "Cambridge Seven," with the most famous being the athlete, C.T. Studd.

Through their influence, many were motivated to give their lives to missions. But something else remarkable happened on this trip. Moody's friends asked him to share an encouraging word as the tour came to an end. Having already preached that day, Moody asked Henry Drummond to share. Drummond pulled out his Bible, turned to 1 Corinthians 13, and shared a message on God's love.

Moody was so moved by this message he asked Drummond to preach it at his church, and then urged him to have it published. The sermon was published, and since that date in 1884, has sold over twelve million copies.[2] Drummond's message has been so widely read because we all need to know God loves us; He loves us like crazy.

**Personalize this: "God loves me like crazy." How should this affect the way you live?**

Zach looked at Nanny with fear, hurt, and anger in his eyes. Zach said what we all think and feel at times: *God, where are you*? *God, why is this happening*? *God, I don't understand*. Life can be tough and confusing, but God is bigger than our difficulties and pain.

**When have you questioned God about a certain situation in your life or where He was during that time?**

Nanny doesn't try to tackle Zach's questions—she goes after his heart. She shares her story: at many points along the way, life was incredibly difficult. She was diagnosed with cancer, dreams failed, she lost friends, but Nanny began to see God's love as life carried on. God has a plan for each of our lives, but He also desires our pain to be eclipsed by the power of His love. Every step along the way, He's with us. No matter how difficult life becomes, God wants us to remember everything is designed to point to our loving Father.

## Christ's Death Is the Proof of God's Love (Rom. 5:8)

We can know God's love because of Christ. Have you ever wondered why Jesus came in the flesh in the first place? Paul gave the reason: God loves us. Maybe you know this verse by heart, but here's John's take: "For God loved the world in this way: He gave his one and only Son, so that everyone who believes in him will not perish but have eternal life" (3:16).

There were some really big implications for Jesus when He came to this world. He stepped down out of heaven and onto earth, took on flesh, and became a man while simultaneously being fully God. Paul tells us that He emptied Himself (Phil. 2:7). This means He lived in our fallen world, endured our pains and weaknesses, was tempted, attacked, betrayed, and mercilessly beaten until the Romans were ready to crucify Him. Jesus' coming from heaven to earth was the Father's plan, and He was willing to go through it because He desired to obey the Father. And He longed to see God's people rescued.

**Jesus gave up everything to rescue you. What might God be calling you to give up to reach out to others?**

Because God is just and sin deserves punishment, payment is required and the price is God's wrath. Isaiah says it pleased God to crush Jesus, and God poured on Jesus the wrath sinful people deserve (Isa. 53:10). This is all a picture of God's love for people. God loved you enough to send Jesus on a rescue mission. Not just the ambiguous masses of people around the world, but you specifically.

**Who is God asking you to share this truth with? How will you do that?**

## Christ Died for Us—Weak, Ungodly, Sinners, and Enemies (Rom. 5:6-10)

Paul describes us as helpless, ungodly, sinners, and enemies. That's not good! We need to regularly take time to consider who we were before Christ saved us. We could never earn our way to Him on our own, so God sent Christ. We were helpless, but He loved us enough to help us. We were ungodly and headed in the wrong direction, and God stepped in to turn us around. We were sinners, yet He cleansed our sin. We were His enemies and on the opposite side of the battle lines, yet He made us family.

**When have you been tempted to think you can work your way into God's grace? How does this passage defeat that idea?**

This applies to everyone—we were all helpless, ungodly, sinners, and enemies until God stepped in and changed everything by sending Jesus to take our place. So, when we say God sent Jesus for us, it's more than just a phrase—it's a full-scale transformation. He did all of this because He loves us.

## Christ's Love Changes Us (Rom. 5:6-11)

Love like this isn't just *difficult* to believe, it's unbelievable! Paul starts off by saying we have now been declared righteous. R.C. Sproul said, "The good news is that God justifies the ungodly freely, by giving to all who believe a righteousness that is not their own."[3] This big phrase basically means God declares us righteous, not based on what we have done, but on what Christ has done. Jesus took our place and took the punishment we deserve. Even more, all of Christ's righteousness is then credited to us.

It's hard to imagine, but it would be like having our maxed out credit cards switched with Bill Gates' debit card. One has debt, and one has a surplus of funds. Dr. Sproul points out that what we possess isn't ours—it's Christ's. Jesus' righteousness is credited to us, and God places it on us like the robe the father placed on the prodigal son. At the moment we trust in Christ, the Father instantly declares us justified and righteous.

Paul takes this idea even further. He looks ahead to the end of time, to the day when God will judge the world and separate the sheep from the goats (Matt. 25:31-46). Because of Christ, we will be spared from judgment. We are instantly declared righteous according to Jesus' death in our place and saved from God's wrath. When Jesus died on the cross, He took our punishment for sin, and we now have nothing to fear. God loved us so much that He was willing to pour out the punishment for sin on Jesus.

**What does this passage teach you about God's wrath and His grace toward believers?**

And as if this isn't enough, Paul says that we've been reconciled to God (v. 10). In fact, Paul uses forms of the word "reconcile" three different times in this passage. Anytime the

Bible uses a phrase three times, it is meant to express the permanence and abundance of the idea. It's like saying holy, holier, holiest in our language. Paul is expressing the perfection of our restored relationship with God. He says we have an unhindered relationship with God. Tim Keller puts it this way, "The only person who dares wake up a king at 3 a.m. for a glass of water is a child. We have that kind of access."[4]

We have been adopted into God's family. We're no longer slaves, but sons and daughters. No longer enemies, but reconciled and made family. We may not always feel like it, but we are loved by God. He proved this love by pursuing us, even when we were dead in sin and deserved His wrath.

**How have you experienced God's love? How should God's consistent love shape the way you live?**

## What is Love? (1 Cor. 13)

We are quick to say we love things in our culture: pizza, football, friends, parents, Jesus. Our culture presses students to think of love in many ways, and it can be confusing. How can we know what love really is?

**Give some examples of what our culture says love is.**

What if, instead of looking at the world around us, we begin looking to God to define love for us? While the world's definition of love is often self-serving, God's love is self-sacrificing. He gives His love freely, even though we've done nothing and can do nothing to deserve it. Brennan Manning says it this way: "My deepest awareness of myself is that I am deeply loved by Jesus Christ and I have done nothing to earn it or deserve it."[5]

**List some ways looking toward His love as the example could change the way you view and express love toward others.**

# [ ON YOUR OWN ]

## DAY 1

## GOD'S LOVE IS BIG

In January 2009, Florida played Oklahoma for the college football national championship. Tim Tebow, Florida's quarterback, had written a verse on his eye black all season: Philippians 4:13. However, just before he ran out on the field and with millions watching around the world, Tim decided to change things up. He wrote John 3:16 instead. Tim prayed that this small gesture would bring glory to God, but had no clue how God would use it. After winning the championship, Coach Urban Meyer told Tim that 94 million people had searched online for John 3:16 during the game.[6] In one sense, this is quite a surprise. However, God's plan from the beginning has been for the world to know His great love.

### God's Original Plan: Love (John 3:16-17)

Jesus talked with Nicodemus about God's big love. From the very beginning, God's design was for the world to know His love. In Genesis 1:28, God commanded Adam and Eve to "be fruitful, multiply." He was calling people—unique in all creation and created in God's image—to spread out so His love would cover the earth.

**What are some practical ways you be part of God's plan to help the world know His love?**

### God's Redemptive Plan: Love (John 3:16-17)

When we rebelled against God, everything changed except God's love. God explained that there would be consequences of the fall (Gen. 3:15), but He also promised to send a Rescuer because of His great love.

**When did you first recognize your need for rescue from sin?**

In Genesis 22:18, God promised Abraham his family would grow in number and that the whole world would know of God's love through them. God would redeem Israel, but His Redeemer was also coming for the rest of the world (Isa. 49:6). Jesus is that promised Redeemer, and He displayed God's big love to the world. God didn't just feel affections for humanity, He acted on His affections. God sent His Only Son, Jesus, on a rescue mission motivated by His big love.

**In your own words, how big is God's love?**

## God's Eternal Plan: Love (John 3:16-17)

Jesus stood before Nicodemus as proof of God's love. God not only created us and sent Jesus because of His love; but further, His plan for all of eternity is that we will continue growing in our knowledge of God and His love. One day, every tongue, tribe, and nation will stand before the Lord (Rev. 7:9). This is a picture of God's fulfilling what He set out to do—to love the world and rescue people from all nations through Abraham's line.

**Because God loves the whole world, no one who is excluded. That includes all races, ethnicities, backgrounds, pasts, sins, and so on. Why do you think this message gets lost?**

God loves all people, including you and me. The question is: How have you responded to His love? His love changes everything, but only for those who respond. Jesus told Nicodemus that, unless someone is born again, he can't enter God's kingdom. Has God's loved changed you? Has it brought you into the kingdom and made you a part of His family?

# DAY 2

## GOD'S LOVE IS SPECIFIC

Jesus came to die as our substitute, to pay our debt, and to love us in a very specific way. In John 6, Jesus told this crowd God sent Jesus to feed them like He sent the manna to the Israelites in the wilderness—He is the bread of life. Jesus wanted them to know God had a specific kind of love for a specific people with a specific purpose.

## A Specific Love (John 6:34-40)

Jesus had fed 5,000 plus people just the day before, and they came back looking for another meal. Jesus used this opportunity make it clear—He's not after their stomachs, but their hearts. They were hungry for food, but Jesus wasn't a chef. He was the Messiah.

**Why do you think the people misunderstood what Jesus meant when He said He is the bread of life?**

God had a specific kind of love for them, a redemptive love. When Jesus declared "I am the bread of life," He meant specifically that He could satisfy their deepest need, which was spiritual. God knew all along we needed a specific kind of love and food for our soul much more than food for our stomachs. We needed to be saved.

## A Specific People (John 6:41-51)

Since the fall, people have always needed a specific kind of love: a saving love. But beyond that, God's redeeming love is for a specific people. Those listening to Jesus didn't fully understand what He meant. And they weren't just confused—they were angry. After all, they knew who Jesus was: Joseph and Mary's son. They wanted a Messiah who did what they wanted—and Jesus did not fit that description. The tension in this passage was caused by people who didn't want His salvation because they wanted things their own way. People have always struggled with Jesus because following Him means we have to admit that we can't save ourselves. God sent Jesus for everyone, but not everyone will be a part of His family. It's a sad fact and a difficult truth, but only those who confess with their mouths and believe in their hearts will be saved (Rom. 10:9).

**Why do you think it's so hard for us to admit that we cannot save ourselves?**

The Bible teaches that before we are saved, we are dead in our trespasses. Yet, while we are lost God loves us and saves us (Rom. 5:8). No one in hell will say God didn't give them a chance to respond to His love and no one in heaven will say that they got there apart from God's sovereignty. It's a mystery that reveals something profound. If you're a believer, you have been loved specifically.

### A Specific Purpose (John 6:52-59)

Jesus once again brings up the illustration of manna, but the bread of life accomplishes something very different. When God's people ate manna, they would become hungry again, and eventually they'd die. But those who feed on the bread of life will never again be hungry, having eternal life with God. Jesus wants them to know that God's specific love met a specific need, and had a specific purpose: to sustain them for eternity. Let's make sure to never forget God's love is immeasurably big. At the same time, don't lose sight of the truth that God has specifically loved you. If you're a Christian, He has chosen you: You are His child, and you will know His love for eternity.

**Only God can save people. How does this take the pressure off as you are sharing your faith?**

# DAY 3

## GOD'S LOVE IS POWERFUL

John 13 tells the story of the Last Supper. Jesus gathered His disciples for one last conversation before His arrest, trial, and crucifixion. Jesus wanted to make sure they knew very clearly how much He loved them and how that love would guide them through the difficulties they would experience. Those difficulties would extend beyond His crucifixion: most of them would give their lives. First, He prepared them, then He prayed for them. Through this conversation, we see a few ways Jesus' love changes us.

### God's Love is Uncontainable (John 13:34a)

Jesus told the disciples He had a new commandment for them: Love one another. The disciples lived in a world of commandments. The Pharisees had over 600 laws they worked diligently to keep, but they still totally missed the point. The Pharisees were so busy keeping all the rules that they never learned to love God. Jesus clarified the purpose of the commandments. It's not about keeping rules but learning to live sacrificially as an expression of love for others, and ultimately, for God.

**When you view God's commands as a way of expressing love for Him and others, how does that affect your motivation to walk in obedience?**

When we experience God's love, it is uncontainable! And when we are marked by God's love, identity, confidence, and purpose, the expressions of these naturally overflow because of the transformation He's brought to our lives. On the other hand, we can't just drum it up if it's not there. If you've been loved by God, you love others.

## God's Love Multiplies (John 13:34b)

For three years, Jesus had taken the disciples with Him everywhere He went. He discipled them, demonstrated how to do ministry, and modeled perfect love. Discipleship is intentionally spending time and doing life with someone in order to see them grow in Christlikeness. Jesus poured into these men so that they could carry forward the message of the gospel after His death, resurrection, and ascension.

Consider Jesus' prayer for the disciples in John 17. Just hours before His crucifixion, Jesus expressed to the Father, " I have glorified you on the earth by completing the work you gave me to do" (v. 4). During His earthly ministry, Jesus lived in complete obedience and fulfilled all the Father had for Him leading up to His death, including preparing the disciples to carry on the gospel work after His departure. Jesus modeled genuine love in such a powerful way that the message and reality of the church has continued even to this day. Jesus multiplied His ministry, so did the disciples, and so will we.

**What is discipleship? How are you growing as a disciple? How can you make disciples?**

## God's Love is Defining (John 13:35)

Lastly, Jesus told them that God's love would define them. The goal was for people to be able to tell something was different about the disciples' lives when they looked at them. They loved each other, they loved the church, and they loved the lost in a such a way that it was easy to see God's love defined them. God's love is transformational; it will motivate us to love others, and this becomes a defining characteristic for all Christ followers. Throughout the Bible, we read stories of God's love transforming people. God's love would ultimately lead Jesus' disciples to give up their lives for the gospel. Today, God's love defines us in the same way.

**What defines you? What would it take for God's love to be the thing that comes to mind when people think about you?**

# SURRENDER

MATTHEW 16:24-26

## WATCH

In this scene, we see Zach surrender to God. Zach had grown up in a religious home, but when his mom passed away, he blamed God. When Zach's dad left, he thought he had even more reason to doubt God's love, yet God consistently pursued Zach with His love and grace. Dave loved Zach and had shared God's love with him. Nanny walked with Zach, pouring her wisdom into his life. Ginger showed Zach patience and simply cared for him as he processed his injuries and the ways they could affect his life. With Dave's new seizure, and Zach's realizing that he's not in control, the love and investment of Dave, Nanny, and Ginger helped to open Zach's eyes to God's love. In this scene, we see Zach surrender to God.

## DISCUSS

God pursues His children with His love. As life happens, God's pursuing us either hardens our hearts as we struggle to exercise control, or we're forced to our knees in surrender. We give up because we can't find the peace we long for, we can't solve our problems, and we can't save ourselves. Our idols and our abilities fail us over and over again, and we're left empty and longing for more every time. God is extremely kind and patient to bring us to the point of surrender.

**When has God brought you to a point of surrender? What was difficult about that situation? What did you learn about God through it?**

Hiroo Onoda was born in Japan in 1922. When World War II broke out, Hiroo was assigned to serve in the Philippines, specifically on the island of Lubang. General MacArthur and the U.S. troops were supporting the Filipino army and supplying resources, so Hiroo and his men were there to fight back, attempting to take the Philippines for Japan. In typical Japanese military fashion, Hiroo was instructed by his superior officer not to surrender. If the enemy overtook them, he was to take his own life. Hiroo and his troops fought hard, but on February 28, 1945, the Filipino and American troops succeeded in securing the island. All the Japanese soldiers were captured or killed except for Hiroo and three of his men who had fled into the jungle to hide.

Four soldiers hiding in the jungles could no longer formally attack an army, so they adapted. In order to survive, and in the continued pursuit of their mission, the soldiers hid deep within the jungles and used guerrilla warfare. Several times over the years, the men found pamphlets announcing the end of the war, and even had an airplane fly over with the message that the ward had ended. However, they thought these were deceptive and an attempt to get them to surrender, so they ignored the messages and continued in their hiding. Eventually one of Hiroo's men left the small group, but Hiroo and the other two were unwilling to give up.

For years, they fought the locals and the local police, until all had died except for Hiroo. In 1974, a Japanese student who had heard stories of the soldier hiding in the jungles set out to find him. Norio Suzuki found Hiroo, but could not convince him that the war was over, so he returned to Japan to find Hiroo's commanding officer. Major Yoshimi Taniguchi had returned to civilian life and was a bookseller. Upon hearing of Hiroo, he flew to Lubang, located Hiroo, and told him that the war had been over since 1945. On March 9, 1972, Hiroo handed over his sword and his rifle, and he finally surrendered.[1]

Much like Hiroo, we are fighting a war that ended long ago—one that's impossible for us to win. Our efforts to maintain control of our lives do nothing but create more problems for us. We need to lay down our weapons and our lives in surrender to the One who is sovereign and victorious.

**What does it mean to surrender to God?**

**In this case, how does surrender actually bring victory?**

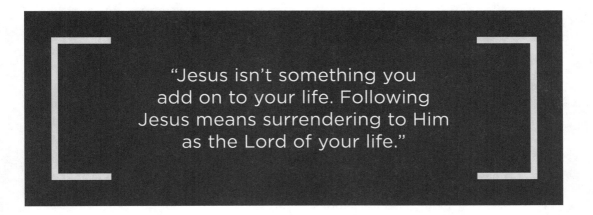

> "Jesus isn't something you add on to your life. Following Jesus means surrendering to Him as the Lord of your life."

Have you ever felt like Zach, and said, "I'm tired of running"? It's easy for many of us to grow up in church, continually be taught the Bible, know all the Sunday school answers, and somehow still miss the point. It's totally possible that you've made it through another Christian movie, another Bible study, or another church service and still missed who Jesus is.

Once, a prisoner of the Prince of Granada remained in jail for 33 years without any companions other than a Bible they had left with him. He studied the Bible intensely. He wrote detailed notes all along the walls, like which verses were the longest and shortest, and how many words the Bible contains. But one of the most fascinating (and tragic) facts is, in all the notes scribbled on the walls, not once did he mention Jesus is Lord.[2] It's totally possible to be in church your whole life, but miss Jesus.

Saying, "I'm tired of running," is Zach's moment of surrender; his way of giving up control. Jesus said it this way:

> *Then Jesus said to his disciples, "If anyone wants to follow after me, let him deny himself, take up his cross, and follow me. For whoever wants to save his life will lose it, but whoever loses his life because of me will find it."*
> **MATTHEW 16:24-25**

Jesus was very clear as He instructed His disciples in Matthew 16. If you've never surrendered and had a moment where you told God, "I'm done running," then it doesn't matter how often you're in church, how much you know about the Bible, or how good you think you are: You're spiritually dead. Jesus isn't something you add on to your life. Following Jesus means surrendering to Him as the Lord of your life.

## Deny Yourself (Matt. 16:24-26)

There is nothing more illogical than giving up, yet, Jesus said "whoever wants to save his life will lose it" (Matt. 16:25). Whether that's in sports, on a test, or in a relationship, giving up is tough because it's contrary to everything that's natural. Nothing in this life tells us losing means winning or dying means living. But here's the problem: continuing to do what we've always done means losing. We may not understand it all, and it may seem at times that religious people are hypocrites or liars, and we may become angry with God like Zach did. In reality, continuing to fight God for control of our lives leads only to greater problems.

**Think of a time in your life when fighting God for control only created more problems. What happened?**

Of course, we all want to save our lives and experience good things, and this starts with denying ourselves. We experience such difficulties because of sin, and this is a problem we can't fix for ourselves. God loves us enough that He sent Jesus to do what we could never do. Denying ourselves means to quit trying to save ourselves, instead surrendering to the One who can.

**What is the difference between good and holy? Why can we never be good enough?**

## Take Up Your Cross (Rom. 10:9-10)

The cross was scandalous, but the cross has somehow become a social symbol— something to be worn or tattooed. In Jesus' day, it was the most torturous and humiliating form of death possible. Jesus says if we want to follow Him, we have to die. Here's what's interesting though. Jesus didn't say we have to be crucified; He said we must take up our cross. Jesus gave this instruction well before He went to the cross to give His life for ours. Therefore, the disciples would not have made the connection. But today we understand that taking up our cross is an act of surrender, giving our lives for something greater.

**List some things you've had to surrender or think you will have to surrender to follow Jesus.**

Paul calls for the same thing in Romans 10. Confessing Jesus is Lord means I need to give the position of lord in my life. Jesus' call to the disciples was a difficult one to process. Denying themselves was one thing, but laying down their lives? There would be no going back from this kind of surrender. Zach surrendered his life because He knew that God loved him and Jesus died for him, but he also knew he couldn't do anything to add to what Jesus had already done. Zach knew his way had failed, so he stopped trying, and he laid down his life. Have you taken up your cross?

## Follow Me (Gal. 2:19-20)

You probably played "Follow the Leader" as a child. It's a simple game: You follow and do whatever the leader does. The complication wasn't how to play the game, but identifying who the leader was. Everyone wanted to be the leader, and it was only fun to follow for so long. Sadly, we still struggle with following. We all want things our way, and we even want others to follow us, doing things our way.

**When do you struggle the most to follow someone or listen to instruction? Why? Explain.**

Jesus' disciples gave up a lot in order to follow Him. But Jesus still said to them, "If anyone wants to follow after me, let him deny himself, take up his cross, and follow me" (Matt. 16:24). Hadn't the disciples been following Him for a long time? I'm sure this was confusing for them, because they'd covered a lot of ground walking with Jesus. In Jesus' day, a Rabbi's invitation to follow was quite an honor. It was an offer to come alongside a respected teacher as a disciple, similar to an apprentice, learning to live as he did. Jesus' words to His disciples were His way of pressing them to do more than just walk alongside Him. Jesus wanted them to join Him on His mission. It's not enough to simply stop doing what we were doing, giving Jesus our lives means living for His glory in every way.

If someone spent a week following you and observing your life, then would they be pointed to God? Paul said, "I have been crucified with Christ, and I no longer live, but Christ lives in me. The life I now live in the body, I live by faith in the Son of God, who loved me and gave himself for me" (Gal. 2:20). Following Jesus means your life belongs to Him: You surrendered your life completely to Him when you trusted in Him to save you. If we're His, our lives should show it.

We are not in control. We are sinners, and there is no way to God except through Jesus. Salvation starts with surrender. Take up your cross. Follow Him. Surrender.

**How does surrendering to Christ make us holy?**

**Have you surrendered to Christ? If not, what's holding you back?**

# [ ON YOUR OWN ]

## Background

Luke was a physician, and he had undertaken the task of investigating Jesus and recording the evidence of who Jesus is for his friend, Theophilus. Luke wrote two volumes for his friend to help him understand what Jesus had done. The Gospel of Luke focuses on Jesus as our sacrifice, and Acts demonstrates how His sacrifices changes the world. Jesus gave His life completely to the Father's will, including dying as our sacrifice on the cross. As we study these passages, we need to consider that we are called to give our lives as well if we are Christ-followers. All three of these passages contain comments from Jesus to those who ask about following Him, and these conversations take place as He is walking to Jerusalem where He will give His life. Following Jesus is all about surrendering.

## DAY 1

### Following Means Surrendering (Luke 9:57-62)

In Luke 9, three different people express to Jesus that they want to follow Him. He responds by asking each person if they've considered the cost. Following Jesus is costly—it means surrendering everything. While God may not call you to give up everything or leave behind everything and everyone familiar, you have to be willing to give up all you have and know—even your own life.

**What has God asked you to give up to follow Him?**

### Surrender Your Comfort (Luke 9:57-58)

The first person says, "I will follow You wherever You go!" Jesus immediately questions this enthusiasm. Are you willing to give up what's comfortable? Jesus was homeless. It's not that He was lazy or wasn't taken care of, but His priorities were completely different than most other people. He was focused on God above all else. We often become fixated on our comfort, but following Jesus means making Him Lord, giving up the things that would draw us away from Him. Followers of Jesus give up comfort because Jesus is better and more precious than anything else in the world.

**Think about what makes you comfortable. What would you do if Jesus asked you to give those things up to follow Him?**

## Surrender Your Obligations (Luke 9:59-60)

The next man asked if he could go and bury his father. There is nothing sinful about taking care of our families. In fact, Jesus commends this in multiple places in the Bible. Jewish customs also saw honoring one's father through the burial process as a serious priority. In fact, this could have taken up to a year.

**If there's nothing sinful about taking care of our families, why do you think Jesus told this man he couldn't bury His father?**

Jesus' point is not that we shouldn't honor or love our families, but that He should be our highest priority. Nothing should be more important to us than Him and His will. We may have several obligations and commitments, but Jesus says nothing is to be more important than Him. Is Jesus your top priority? If not, you haven't surrendered.

## Surrender Your Everything (Luke 9:61-62)

The last man just wanted to say goodbye to friends and family. It's not that Jesus wants us to be anti-social and anti-familial. Jesus' point here is that it's all or nothing. There's a story told of Charlemagne, a Christian who was the first emperor of Western-Europe following the fall of the Roman Empire. He wanted all his soldiers to be saved, so he baptized them all. The church in the middle ages taught that this was how you were converted. There was one problem, the soldiers had to fight and kill in battle, so when they were baptized in the river, everything would go under the water except for their sword hand. This way they would be free to kill. That sounds crazy, right? That's exactly what Jesus is saying here. Jesus obviously knew what was in this man's heart. This wasn't a request; it was a statement. The man was willing to give Jesus some, but not all.

Following Jesus means surrendering everything. You give up anything that would take priority over Him. It truly is all or nothing.

**Why is Jesus seemingly so harsh in some of His responses? What do you think these three people heard Him say? What did you hear Him say?**

# DAY 2

## Surrendering is Costly (Luke 14:25-33)

In the verses before this passage, Jesus described a banquet and how all those invited had excuses for not attending. The point is that the Messiah was there, yet they were all busy with other things. Isn't that true of us? How many times have you said something like, "I would read my Bible more if I had more time"? If you haven't said it out loud, have you said it with your actions?

**If surrendering means giving your life to God, does your daily schedule reflect that He is Lord? If not, what changes can you make to spend more time with God?**

## Surrendering Your Relationships (Luke 14:25-26)

Jesus uses some very strong words here to say that we aren't to love anyone, including our families, more than Him. It's a question of priority. Who are the people closest to you? Who are the people that influence you the most? Relationships require time and investment. Jesus was asking what would keep you from Him. No matter the relationship, if anyone keeps you from Him, changes must be made. Surrendering to Jesus means your relationship with Him is the most important relationship you have. Ironically, loving Jesus supremely means you will love your family, friends, and the lost more. Surrendering to Jesus will cost you certain relationships, but it will enrich others.

**What relationships do you have that press you towards God? What relationships do you have that pull you away from God? What should you do about both?**

## Surrendering Your Future (Luke 14:27)

Taking up your cross means literally walking to your death. We can dress this statement up in comfy Christian terms, but Jesus' audience heard exactly what He was saying. Following Jesus means dying. By this, He is asking what we are really living for. Just as relationships might get in the way of following Jesus, so might our plans for our lives.

We can completely map out our lives (college, career, marriage, and so on) and none of it be about God. Like the people who turned down the banquet, we can stay busy every single day, even with good things, but if we're not focused on God moment by moment, we haven't surrendered. We can't be His disciples if our lives are about us. Surrendering to Jesus will cost the future.

**What are your plans for your future? Where does God fit into those plans?**

## Surrendering Your Stuff (Luke 14:33)

In order to take up your cross, you have to put some things down. What do you own that you love? Maybe it's your clothes, your car, a guitar or gaming system. Jesus says if we're not careful, instead of owning stuff, our stuff will own us. We work to buy things, live to enjoy them, we fight for them. It's possible we do all these things because our possessions are idols, as Jesus said, we can't serve two masters (Luke 16:13). Charles Spurgeon said that an idol is, "Whatever we sin to gain, (or) whatever we sin to keep."

Who do you serve? What owns your heart? Surrendering to Jesus costs us our stuff because it means surrendering our hearts. Surrendering to Jesus means loving Him to the point that nothing else matters. This is why Jesus tells us to take time to consider these things. Just like a building requires serious planning, and going to war requires intentional strategy, we need to think clearly about our hearts.

**Can you think of anything in your life that might be an idol? How can you deal with that?**

## DAY 3

## Being Good Is Not Surrendering (Luke 18:18-27)

*Surrender* is a military word, and we can't surrender if we don't understand we're in a battle. Life is happening non-stop, and most people in the world are so caught up in what's right in front of them that few stop to consider where it's all heading. The rich young ruler is a perfect example of this. He was a real person who had an encounter with Jesus. But what we see is someone so caught up in his own story that he didn't realize what really matters: who he was himself, who God is, or that there could be something bigger in life. Jesus warned that if we don't look beyond our own lives to the ultimate reality—God—we have no hope.

**Why do you think most people think they are good enough to go to heaven? What do many people see as the standard for "good enough"? What's the true standard?**

## You Can't Earn It (Luke 18:18-23)

Seventy-two percent of Americans say they believe in heaven, and when asked how to get there many said, heaven is "where people who have led good lives are eternally rewarded." The rich young ruler by his very question, "What must *I do*," (emphasis mine) demonstrates that he assumed salvation was something to be earned. This is why Jesus questioned him, "Why do you call me good?" Jesus was confronting the man's ideas of right and wrong, good and bad, and showing him that only God is good enough to secure salvation for His people. We surrender because we can't earn. There is no such thing as good enough—there is only Jesus. Don't make this life about you, and what you do or don't do. Make it about Jesus.

**What would you say if someone asked you "What must I do to inherit eternal life?"?**

## You Can't Add it On (Luke 18:24-27)

The problem is that most of us treat God as an add-on to our lives. But God won't share the throne with anyone or anything. Jesus took the time to point out to the crowd that we can't simply add God to our lives, we have to surrender. Then we'll experience that "What is impossible with man is possible with God." Did you catch what Jesus said? It's impossible for men to save themselves. There is no such thing as good enough. The rich young ruler was probably very moral. After all, he claimed to have kept all the laws from his youth.

The issue isn't how good we are. It's about being holy, and no one can live up to that standard. This is why Jesus came in our place—God alone is holy. God has made a way, and what was impossible before is now possible because of Jesus, but it can't simply be added on. We have to give up all our old ways the live in Him.

**What does it mean to surrender to God? Why is this so important?**

# LIFE ON MISSION

MATTHEW 28:19-20

# WATCH

In this scene, we see that God's plan for Zach was bigger than he recognized. Despite Dave's injuries, God used him to save Zach's dream of getting out of Bessemer and to save Zach's soul. Zach owes everything to God, but he also owes a lot to Dave because Dave pointed him to God.

# DISCUSS

We should all want to be like Dave—loving and leading others to know Jesus. God has called us to live for His glory and in such a way that others know He is good. Does your life honor God this way? When we live for God, our lives have an eternal impact by the ways we live, speak, and love others. We've been saved to proclaim the gospel in all we do and say to everyone we meet.

**Who in your life should you be pursuing with God's love?**

When we think about examples of people who devoted their lives to God's purposes, several names may come to mind; men and women like the apostle Paul, William Carey, Adoniram Judson, Lottie Moon, Hudson Taylor, Amy Carmichael, Jim Elliott, Count Zinzendorf, the Moravians, or even St. Patrick. The Christian faith is filled with believers who have taken their faith to the ends of the earth for the purpose of loving others and sharing the gospel.

**What does it look like for you to live on mission?**

The frontier world of the 1700s was one marked by war and attacks between the French, Native Americans, and the English settlers. Jonathan Edwards, a pastor from Massachusetts, lost multiple family members in one of these attacks, and he also had many friends that were killed or taken captive in various battles. In spite of the pain and fear, Edwards and his family moved to Stockbridge, Massachusetts in 1751 to join the work of educating, building relationships, and ministering to the Mahican Indians.[1] God used Edwards in a powerful way in this season, while helping him to learn and grow, and Edwards wrote several of his most important works during that time.

The Lord is calling each of us to *go* for His glory. It may mean going around the world or across the street. God may be calling us to serve people we've never met or loving our enemies. We go to others because Jesus came to us.

**Why is it sometimes difficult to share our faith?**

## LIVING FOR GOD

Have you ever asked yourself what God wants for your life? One of the most important things we can know is this: God has a plan for each of our lives. We aren't just bouncing around aimlessly; we were made by God and for God. So, the next logical question is: What is that purpose? Salvation happens in an instant. One second we are lost, enemies of God, rebels to His will, and dead spiritually. Then in a moment, everything changes. We are adopted, children of God, lovers of His Word, and alive to live for Him.

**What does it look like to live for God in your daily life?**

As the movie ends, Zach reflects on Dave's life. Dave had become his hero because he lived in such a way that God was glorified and Zach was loved. As Zach moves forward, he realizes everything is different because Dave was a part of his life. God wants us to know Him and to help others come to know Him. God wants us to wake up every morning knowing we are loved and forgiven, and that He's empowering us to do bold things for His glory. In a way, God wants us all to be more like Dave.

Imagine the confusion the disciples must have felt after the crucifixion. They had devoted three years of their lives to following Jesus and learning from Him. Then, everything changed drastically. The Romans arrested, beat, crucified, and buried Jesus. The man they had seen do powerful things, like raising Lazarus from the dead, was in a tomb Himself. They were surely hopeless, but then they heard that Jesus wasn't in the tomb. In fact, He was alive.

**What do you think you would have felt if you were in the disciples' place? How would you have responded?**

"We were made to know God, to live for God, to share our lives with others."

It's easy to feel their confusion, but can you imagine their excitement? The disciples were blessed to see the resurrected Jesus a handful of times, and one of those helped clear up any remaining confusion:

> Jesus came near and said to them, "All authority has been given to me in heaven and on earth. Go, therefore, and make disciples of all nations, baptizing them in the name of the Father and of the Son and of the Holy Spirit, teaching them to observe everything I have commanded you. And remember, I am with you always, to the end of the age."
> **MATTHEW 28:18-20**

Jesus' message to His disciples, and to all of us today, is this: "I have a purpose for your life." It's not ambiguous. It's not confusing. We were made to know God, to live for God, to share our lives with others.

## APPLY

### Communion with Jesus (John 17:4)

The last three years of Jesus' ministry had built to this moment. To understand what Jesus said to His disciples before ascending, we have to understand what He prayed in John 17:4. Jesus prayed for the disciples before His arrest, trial, and crucifixion, saying:

> I have glorified you on the earth by completing the work you gave me to do.
> **JOHN 17:4**

Jesus was saying He had finished the work the Father had for Him. All that remained was to give His life as a sacrifice. Here's what this means: While Jesus came to be our substitute, His work was also to make disciples who would carry His message around the world. Before He paid for their sins, Jesus spent time with the disciples, shared meals with them, and taught them. They had seen Jesus perform unbelievable miracles, and they had listened as He shared His heart with them for three years.

**What does it mean to enjoy God? How do you commune with God?**

Before we can understand the things God is calling us to do, we must first understand that God is calling us to Himself. God doesn't want there to be confusion about His love for you: He is crazy about you! You're probably familiar with the idea of communion as something we do at church, but perhaps you're not familiar with what it really means. The Merriam-Webster Dictionary says communion is sharing; it is intimate fellowship.[2] God enjoys spending time with you and has deep affections for you as His child; He wants you to feel the same way about Him. Pastor John Piper said it this way, "God is most glorified in us when we are most satisfied in Him."[3]

**Have you ever thought the fact that God wants you to enjoy Him and His presence in your life? How does this surprise you or make you think differently about God?**

God isn't obligated to save any of us, and our salvation isn't based on anything we've done, so why save any of us? It's because He loves us. Anything we could ever do for God and His kingdom starts here. We aren't earning God's love: We are responding to it. Before Jesus ever commissioned the disciples, He communed with them.

**How have you responded to God's love? In what was has this study affected your response to Him?**

## Go (Matt. 28:19)

Our lives are defined by this tiny, two letter word: *go*. Jesus had no new insights for the eleven men who had followed Him for three years. He simply wanted them to continue doing what He modeled for them. Jesus used everyday situations to turn the world upside down, and He was calling His followers to do the same.

When we think about God's call on our lives, maybe we're afraid God will call us to a foreign land. While this could be the case, it's more likely He is calling us to be faithful in our current situation. Everywhere we go, we have work to do, so we should be continually aware of the opportunities to share the gospel at home, in our neighborhoods and schools, and everywhere else we. This is what it means to *go*.

**Think about your life right now. What opportunities has God given you to share the gospel right where you are?**

Living missionally requires us to be aware that God made us to know Him and make Him known. This means we need always to be conscious of who is around, know they are watching, and see the opportunity to impact their lives. Dave was aware that Zach was always watching, so he waited for opportunities to actively speak truth into Zach's life. For you, it could be a family member, a neighbor, a student in your class, or a waitress at a restaurant. Living sent means engaging every situation as an ambassador for God. We can change the world for God's glory, and it starts with being faithful where we are.

## Make Disciples (Matt. 28:19-20)

Jesus called His disciples to make disciples. It was a commission to do all over the world what He had done with them. Making a disciple can seem like a really complicated task, and you might think it should be left to the experts. I bet that's exactly what the disciples thought too. But making disciples isn't about being an expert, it's about following Jesus, and allowing others to follow our example. Jesus didn't focus on teaching the disciples all the hotly debated matters of doctrine. He spent three years doing life with these men, modeling what it means to live for God's purposes. We'd all do well to identify others we can pour our lives into.

**Jesus said we are saved to make disciples—who are you walking with? If you aren't being discipled or discipling anyone now, who can you find to do both of those things?**

Jesus gave two directives for disciples: We are to baptize and teach. Baptism is an ordinance of the church, which means it's something Jesus commanded as a defining practice for the church. Preaching the Bible, baptism, the Lord's Supper, and church discipline (to a degree) are the marks of a biblical church.[4]

When people come to saving faith in Jesus, the next step is to be baptized, which is an act of expressing publicly our devotion to Jesus. As Christ's followers, we are to lead people to faith and then to take the step of baptism—their publicly professing their faith. But it doesn't stop there. We are then called to teach them all that Jesus has commanded. We are to help others grow to a mature understanding of God's truth. It's not about being an expert, but to help others grow, we must be devoted to growing ourselves. This is why communion with God is so important. As you spend time with God in His Word, in prayer, and with His people at church, you will grow; then you can share what you learn with others.

## Remember (Matt. 28:20)

If you're at this point and you're feeling overwhelmed, that's okay. Changing the world is no small thing. This is why Jesus tells the disciples He has all authority, and He is with them all the way. When people are saved, it's not us doing the saving. When they grow, it's not because of us. Jesus is the One who transforms, and we simply point others to Him. However, God has chosen to use us to accomplish His plan, and it should cause wonder and excitement to see how He will work through us.

**Share about a time when God has used you to point others to Him.**

God has a wonderful plan for every life, and Dave's faithfulness serves as a great example. The plan is not complicated. We're simply called to know God, trust and obey Him, and tell of His goodness to anyone who will listen.

**How could you personally live on mission where you are? Who needs you like Zach needed Dave?**

**What does it mean to you that Jesus has all authority and is with you always?**

The Book of Acts is this beautiful picture of the gospel, the good news of Christ's work, expanding to the ends of the earth. It's the second part of Luke's letter to Theophilus where he shows his friend not just what Jesus did, but how the world is being changed by this Jesus. Acts operates in the New Testament like the Book of Joshua in the Old Testament: Believers are taking the land for the Lord. Through their living, speaking, and loving, we see the nations rejoicing. The entire Book of Acts is summed up in one verse: Acts 1:8. This verse shows Acts as the message of Jesus moving in Jerusalem (Acts 1:1-8:3), to Judea and Samaria (Acts 8:4-12:25), and to the ends of the earth (Acts 13:1-28:31).

## DAY 1

### Living Your Faith (Acts 1:8)

As Dietrich Bonhoeffer said, "when Christ calls a man, he bids him come and die."[5] That might sound heavy, but when we consider the man who said it and how he lived, it makes sense. Bonhoeffer was a faithful man who found himself living in a time when faithfulness was risky. As Hitler took over Germany, few stood in his way, but Bonhoeffer was one of the few who defied the Fuhrer. He was forced to take his ministry underground. With the Nazi's bearing down on him, Bonhoeffer wrote his prolific work, *The Cost of Discipleship* in 1937. He was arrested and imprisoned in 1943 for his faith, and was executed on April 9, 1945—just 14 days before Americans liberated the camp where he was imprisoned.[6]

Although you might not literally have to give up your life for the gospel, we must be prepared to do so. As Jesus gave His life for ours, Christians have given our lives to Him—no matter the cost.

**What's your reaction to the truth that your life belongs to Christ, no matter the cost?**

### Faithfulness May Be Tough

Faithfulness comes with a price. Jesus told those gathered before His ascension, "you will be my witnesses" (Acts 1:8). The Greek word for witness, *martus*, is where we get our word *martyr*. Jesus' statement would prove to be prophetic as the apostles would all be martyred (killed for their faith), except John who died while in exile.

The Lord calls us to live for Him, and that sometimes means things will be difficult. Faithfully living for God may mean missing out on some social events, not dating a specific person, or giving up friends who live in ways contrary to the gospel. It may make you the odd person out in your home. Faithfulness isn't always fun, but it is always right.

**When have you experienced some of the less "fun" aspects of living out your faith?**

**Would you consider yourself faithful? What does faithfulness look like in your life?**

## Tough Isn't Wrong

It's often tough to be faithful because our flesh is weak. It's tough because the world isn't moving toward God but is celebrating sin and rebellion instead. It's tough because we have an enemy who seeks our destruction. Faithfulness is a fight, but the good news is that we aren't alone in that fight.

Jesus says, "but you will receive power when the Holy Spirit has come on you" (Acts 1:8). God hasn't just called us to live faithfully, He has given us the Holy Spirit to help us live faithfully. Experiencing difficult things doesn't mean we're doing things wrong, God doesn't love us, or we need to give up. Tough things let us know we're going against the grain and that we are being made more like Jesus. We should live faithfully, even when it hurts, because the Lord is with us every step of the way. Despite the pain, the Lord uses all our faithful deeds to glorify Himself. Live faithfully because others are watching, and they will see Christ in us.

**Repenting is when we understand we've failed, we confess our failures, and turn to faithfully follow God. When was the last time you repented? If repentance is the first step in faithfulness, what do you need to repent of right now?**

## DAY 2
### Sharing Your Faith (Acts 1:8)

Being a witness in Jerusalem, Judea, and Samaria meant those with Jesus would have to share their faith. But sharing can be very intimidating. LifeWay Research found that 80 percent of those who attend church one or more times a month believe they have a personal responsibility to share their faith. On the flip side, only 39 percent have told another person about how to become a Christian in the previous six months.[7] We have to change this statistic. We need to share our faith.

**Who can you share the gospel with this week?**

## Sharing the Good News

It can be difficult to know exactly what to share. One of the most helpful tools for sharing our faith is the Three Circles model. Jimmy Scroggins and his church came up with a "Life Conversations" model that involves three circles. The first circle has inside it "God's Design," because God has a design for life and a plan for our lives. But we all depart from God's design and do things our way instead of God's way. This is sin, which leads to the second circle, "Brokenness." We are all trying to figure out how to deal with our pain, and that produces even more brokenness unless the way we deal with it the right way—belief and repentance. These are key components of the "Gospel," the third circle. The gospel is God's plan to repair our brokenness. God sent His Son Jesus to live in our place, die in our place for our sins, and rise again as our substitute. When we repent and believe in Jesus, we experience redemption and restoration, which leads back to the first circle, God's original design. This model serves as a conversation guide as you are sharing with someone.

**How do you think the Three Circles model would help you share the gospel?**

**Have you used the 3 Circles model before? If not, what have you used to share your faith? What works? What didn't work?**

SIN

GOD'S
DESIGN

BROKENNESS

RECOVER
AND
PURSUE

GOSPEL

REPENT
AND
BELIEVE

## Loving the Lost

Evangelism isn't necessarily to be a spontaneous event. There are times we should share our faith on the spot with no relationship and potentially no follow-up. However, this isn't the primary way to go about sharing. It's more common to share our faith with someone we know. As you spend time with each other, talking and listening, it's important to notice opportunities to love and encourage them, as well as opportunities to share.

Where someone experiences brokenness, there's a perfect opportunity to explain how it can be fixed according to God's plan. For the disciples, they began sharing in Jerusalem, then things spilled out from there to the surrounding region of Judea and Samaria. As Acts shows, the gospel kept spreading, and is still being carried to the ends of the earth. Today, we are responsible to continue spreading the gospel, so let's not allow fear to rob us of the privilege of being used for God's purposes.

**Who comes to mind right now that you should share your faith with? How can you get some one-on-one time with them to talk to them about Jesus? What will you say?**

## Taking Your Faith (Acts 1:8)

There are nearly 7.5 billion people in the world, but only around 31 percent of them are professing Christians. This means that around 5.25 billion people in the world are lost, and this is an extremely generous estimate. There are nearly 2 billion Muslims, over a billion Hindus, and around half a billion Buddhists, all worshiping false gods.[8]

On top of this, there are hundreds of smaller religions, cults, and the rising movement in the millennial and younger generations toward atheism and agnosticism. These false religions are designed by Satan to keep people trapped in thinking they need to earn their salvation. But there is hope in Jesus, and He told His followers the nations are His goal and the world is our mission.

**What can you do today to join God in His movement around the world?**

## Our Part to Play

We, as God's children, have a part in this work. It's easy to feel like this is out of reach. It seems like the nations are simply beyond us, yet the Lord has told us it's our responsibility to spread His glory to the ends of the earth. No matter the distance and difficulty, we can make a difference today.

As a member of a local church, you can be a part of the work that your church is doing to advance the gospel to the ends of the earth. You can sponsor a child through a ministry like Compassion, giving them a chance to be fed and educated and to hear about Jesus. You can encourage and support a missionary or missionary family. You can go on a trip overseas. You can tap into organizations like the Joshua Project or the International Missions Board to learn about unreached people groups and ways you can pray for them. The point is: God will use you when you make yourself available. Don't buy the lie that you can't do anything. Do something.

**Do you know any missionaries? How could you encourage them? How could your church encourage them?**

## Our Mission to Go

When Jesus called His followers to go to the ends of the earth, where we live today was beyond their comprehension. But because they went, we know of the gospel today. Now, we have a responsibility to go. Today, the nations are coming to America, and we can impact the ends of the earth by loving our neighbors.

Further, the internet allows us to engage the world in ways that weren't possible just a few years ago. It's not a matter of ability, but of willingness. Through you, God will change the world. We have a call to take our faith to the ends of the earth—what part will you play in God's global mission?

**Have you ever been on a mission's trip? Where did you go? If not, how could you start saving money and preparing to go on one soon?**

# LEADER GUIDE

# SESSION 1

Begin by welcoming the group and distributing books to students.

## ◼ BREAK THE ICE (Optional)

If you've ever been to a summer camp, it's likely you've participated in a trust fall. Here's how it works—you climb on top of a platform while your friends stand behind you on the ground with their arms locked. You then turn your back to them, crossing your arms in front of you, and fall back.

Here's the beauty of this exercise: As you fall back, people catch you. It's a silly exercise in trust, but here's the bigger picture: This exercise teaches us that, when we fall, we have people we can trust who will help. You will blow it at some point. You will feel like you have been punched in the mouth. Who will be there to help you get up? Who would you call if your life fell apart right now? Who would call you?

**Make a list of the people you would call, and consider why you put those names on your list. What makes them trustworthy? How can you be more trustworthy?**

**How can we grow in our trust of God and His goodness?**

## ◼ WATCH

Use the Watch section on page 9 to set the stage for the clip from *Run the Race* you're about to view as a group. Then press play on the clip for Session 1.

## ◼ DISCUSS

Use the content and questions in this section to review the video and discuss the group Bible study content for this session.

## ◼ APPLY

Use the questions in this section to review the group content before closing your time together. The purpose of this section is to help students apply what they've learned.

## ◼ ON YOUR OWN

Remind students to complete the personal studies on pages 14-19. Be sure to complete these studies as well so you can review them with students during next week's group time.

# SESSION 2

Begin by welcoming the group and reviewing the personal studies from last week.

## ■ BREAK THE ICE (Optional)

**What is sin? (An Experiment)**
A classic definition of sin is *missing the mark*. It's the picture of an archer shooting his arrow and not even hitting the target.

- If you have access to a basketball hoop, invite a student to shoot 25 free throws. (If you don't have access to a basketball goal, go the cheap route and invite him to throw paper balls from across the room into a small trash can.) How many did you make? How many did you miss? If you were given the rest of your life to only work on shooting free throws, do you think you could perfectly shoot free throws?

- Holiness refers to being morally pure—complete perfection. Ask: Can you think of something you would describe as pure (not necessarily in the moral sense)?

   **Is sin really a big deal? Why or why not?**

   **When compared with a biblical standard, our hearts are not pure. How can they be purified?**

## ■ WATCH
Use the Watch section on page 21 to set the stage for the clip from *Run the Race* you're about to view as a group. Then press play on the clip for Session 2.

## ■ DISCUSS
Use the content and questions in this section to review the video and discuss the group Bible study content for this session.

## ■ APPLY
Use this section to review the group content before closing your time together. The purpose of this section is to help students apply what they've learned as they go into the next week.

## ■ ON YOUR OWN
Remind students to complete the personal studies on pages 27-31. Be sure to complete these studies as well so you can review them with students during next week's group time.

# SESSION 3

Begin by welcoming the group and reviewing the personal studies from last week.

## BREAK THE ICE (Optional)

### The Domino Effect

Set up dominoes so the group can knock them down. Place them in unique and creative patterns to see the domino effect. Talk about the chain reactions—how one thing causes another thing to happen. Teach your group that dominoes can actually knock over something one and a half times their size. Then, with a standard domino as the start, tell them that it would only take 29 dominoes in increasing time-and-a-half sizes to knock over the empire state building! It's not just a chain reaction—it's a multiplying impact! Think about the multiplying domino effect of forgiving someone.

**What does God's forgiving us entail? What does it mean to be forgiven by God?**

**What happens when we forgive someone? When you're forgiven?**

**What could change if you started to forgive people who have hurt you?**

## WATCH

Use the Watch section on page 33 to set the stage for the clips from *Run the Race* you're about to view as a group. Then press play and show both clips for Session 3.

## DISCUSS

Use the content and questions in this section to review the videos and discuss the group Bible study content for this session.

## APPLY

Use this section to review the group content before closing your time together. The purpose of this section is to help students apply what they've learned as they go into the next week.

## ON YOUR OWN

Remind students to complete the personal studies on pages 39-43. Be sure to complete these studies as well so you can review them with students during next week's group time.

# SESSION 4

Begin by welcoming the group and reviewing the personal studies from last week.

## ▪ BREAK THE ICE (Optional)

Provide various magazines, a list of popular television shows, movies, songs, and so on for students to go through. Instruct students to search through the magazines and lists and name as many references to love or quotes about love as they can find. The goal is to have not just lots of options, but to discuss what's relevant in their world. Once students have written out or collected these references, ask them share it with the rest of the group. Then, ask students the following questions.

**What does this say about love?**

**Is this love?**

**How do you think God's love is different?**

## ▪ WATCH

Use the Watch section on page 45 to set the stage for the clip from *Run the Race* you're about to view as a group. Then press play on the clip for Session 4.

## ▪ DISCUSS

Use the content and questions in this section to review the video and discuss the group Bible study content for this session.

## ▪ APPLY

Use this section to review the group content before closing your time together. The purpose of this section is to help students apply what they've learned as they go into the next week.

## ▪ ON YOUR OWN

Remind students to complete the personal studies on pages 51-55. Be sure to complete these studies as well so you can review them with students during next week's group time.

# SESSION 5

Begin by welcoming the group and reviewing the personal studies from last week.

## ▊ BREAK THE ICE (Optional)

Bring several classic board games and have a game night with your students. Many of these games or concepts of these games will be unfamiliar to them, having grown up immersed in the world of cell phones and digital games. Board games are a great way to get them to interact with each other and laugh together.

But let's add a fun catch to game night: whoever loses should formally surrender to the winner. If it's a multiplayer game like Monopoly, all contestants must surrender to whoever bankrupted them. Make a big deal about it—they have to stand up and declare aloud that they are surrendering to the one who has defeated them. Then, they must become the cheerleader for the one they've surrendered to. If the person they've surrendered to loses, they become a cheerleader for the new winner, and so on. If you want to speed this up, you can play cards instead of board games or set a time limit and whoever is ahead when time expires is the winner.

**Is it difficult to surrender in front of everyone? What did surrendered people do? How do you think that relates to our walks with God?**

## ▊ WATCH
Use the Watch section on page 57 to set the stage for the clip from *Run the Race* you're about to view as a group. Then press play on the clip for Session 5.

## ▊ DISCUSS
Use the content and questions in this section to review the video and discuss the group Bible study content for this session.

## ▊ APPLY
Use this section to review the group content before closing your time together. The purpose of this section is to help students apply what they've learned as they go into the next week.

## ▊ ON YOUR OWN
Remind students to complete the personal studies on pages 63-67. Be sure to complete these studies as well so you can review them with students during next week's group time.

# SESSION 6

Begin by welcoming the group and reviewing the personal studies from last week.

## ▢ BREAK THE ICE (Optional)

### Above the Noise

Students will be sharing their faith with friends who will have lots of "noise" in their lives. This activity is designed to help students understand this reality. This activity requires a Communicator and a Listener. Instruct the Communicator to write out a sentence at least ten words long on a piece of paper only they can see. Tell both students to face each other while everyone else (including you) forms a circle around them. Allow one minute for the Communicator to share his or her message with the listener while the rest of the group seeks to distract by talking, yelling, and so on. The students in the circle cannot touch the students in the center. When the 60 seconds pass, ask the Listener to try and share exactly what the Communicator had written down. Select multiple pairs, make it a competition, and give prizes if you'd like. The goal is to get above the "noise" as we seek to share with our friends. When the activity is complete, ask:

> **What was the most frustrating part of being a communicator?**

> **What was the most frustrating part of being a listener?**

## ▢ WATCH

Use the Watch section on page 69 to set the stage for the clip from *Run the Race* you're about to view as a group. Then press play on the clip for Session 6.

## ▢ DISCUSS

Use the content and questions in this section to review the video and discuss the group Bible study content for this session.

## ▢ APPLY

Use this section to review the group content before closing your time together. The purpose of this section is to help students apply what they've learned as they go into the next week.

## ▢ ON YOUR OWN

Remind students to complete the personal studies on pages 75-79. Be sure to complete these studies as well so you can review them with students during next week's group time.

# Sources

## SESSION 1

1. "16 trapped upside-down on roller coaster," January 1, 2008, http://www.china.org.cn/english/China/237690.htm, accessed January 4, 2019.

## SESSION 2

1. Morgan Friedman, The Inflation Calculator, https://westegg.com/inflation/infl.cgi, accessed January 4, 2019.

2. IMDb, Intervention awards, https://www.imdb.com/title/tt0450920/awards, accessed January 4, 2019.

3. Cindy Boren, "'I think you just saved my life': A Bears player en route to camp rescues a choking man," *The Washington Post,* July 24, 2017, https://www.washingtonpost.com/news/early-lead/wp/2017/07/24/i-think-you-just-saved-my-life-a-bears-players-trip-to-training-camp-was-anything-but-ordinary/?utm_term=.84cfae7ec0b6, accessed January 4, 2019.

4. Timothy Keller, *The Prodigal God: Recovering the Heart of the Christian Faith* (New York: Penguin Books, 2008), 36.

5. Rembrandt van Rijn: Biography and Chronology, http://www.rembrandtpainting.net/rembrandt_life_and_work.htm, accessed January 4, 2019.

## SESSION 3

1. Tori Peglar, "1995 Reintroduction of Wolves in Yellowstone," July 9, 2018, https://www.yellowstonepark.com/park/yellowstone-wolves-reintroduction, accessed January 4, 2019.

2. Reference: Avalanches, "Types of Avalanches," *National Geographic,* https://www.nationalgeographic.com/environment/natural-disasters/avalanches/, accessed January 4, 2019.

3. NOAA Office of Response and Restoration, "What Does the Sahara Desert Have to Do with Hurricanes?", August 24, 2014, https://response.restoration.noaa.gov/about/media/what-does-sahara-desert-have-do-hurricanes.html, accessed January 4, 2019.

4. John R.W. Stott, *The Cross of Christ,* 20th ed. (Downers Grove, IL: IVP Books, 2006), 158.

5. The Church of Eleven 22, Vimeo, "The Riches of His Grace: Ike Brown's Story," https://vimeo.com/160777995, accessed January 4, 2019.

6. Travis M. Andrews & Lindsey Bever, "'My pipe dream finally came true': This woman won the second-largest Powerball jackpot ever," *The Washington Post,* August 24, 2017, https://www.washingtonpost.com/news/morning-mix/wp/2017/08/24/the-second-largest-jackpot-in-powerball-history-has-a-winner/?utm_term=.a4db4440a17f, accessed January 4, 2019.

7. Robert Kaylor, "The Gospel in Three Phrases," https://www.seedbed.com/untitled-34/, accessed January 4, 2019.

## SESSION 4

1. "Transcript: Read Kurt Warner's Hall of Fame speech," *The Gazette,* August 6,2017, https://www.thegazette.com/subject/sports/transcript-read-kurt-warners-hall-of-fame-speech-20170806, accessed January 4, 2019.

2. Jesus Fellowship, "Henry Drummond," https://jesus.org.uk/book_author/henry-drummond/, accessed January 4, 2019.

3. R.C. Sproul, Ligonier Ministries (@ligonier), Twitter, November 19, 2013, https://twitter.com/Ligonier/statuses/402832555273383936, accessed January 4, 2019.

4. Timothy Keller (@timkellernyc), Twitter, February 23, 2015, https://twitter.com/timkellernyc/status/569890726349307904?lang=en, accessed January 4, 2019.

5. Brennan Manning, *The Ragamuffin Gospel,* (Colorado Springs, CO: Multonomah Books, 2015), 11.

6. Terry Douglass, "Former Heisman winner Tebow headlines FCA event in G.I.," *The Grand Island Independent,* April 16, 2015, https://www.theindependent.com/sports/former-heisman-winner-tebow-headlines-fca-event-in-g-i/article_83d125d6-e4c0-11e4-9134-07f3b545a2be.html, accessed January 4, 2019.

## SESSION 5

1. Robert D. McFadden, *The New York Times,* January 17, 2014, https://www.nytimes.com/2014/01/18/world/asia/hiroo-onoda-imperial-japanese-army-officer-dies-at-91.html, accessed January 4, 2019.

2. Onward Magazine, April 4, 1903, 111, https://books.google.com/books?id=v8kpAAAAYAAJ&printsec=frontcover&source=gbs_ge_summary_r&cad=0#v=onepage&q=-skull&f=false.

## SESSION 6

1. George M. Marsden, *A Short Life of Jonathan Edwards* (Grand Rapids, MI: Eerdmans, 2008), 118-119.

2. Merriam-Webster, communion, https://www.merriam-webster.com/dictionary/communion, accessed January 4, 2019.

3. John Piper, *Desiring God: Meditations of a Christian Hedonist,* [10th anniversary expanded ed. (Sisters, Or.: Multnomah Books, 1996), 50.

4. Mark Dever, *The Church: The Gospel Made Visible* (Nashville, TN: B&H Academic, 2012), 95.

5. Dietrich Bonhoeffer, *The Cost of Discipleship* (New York: Simon and Schuster, 2012), 11.

6. Wikipedia, "Dietrich Bonhoeffer," https://en.wikipedia.org/wiki/Dietrich_Bonhoeffer, accessed January 4, 2019.

7. Alex Murashko, "Study: Churchgoers Say Sharing Faith Essential, Many Never Do," August 15, 2012, *Christian Post,* https://www.christianpost.com/news/study-churchgoers-say-sharing-faith-essential-many-never-do.html, accessed January 4, 2019.

8. Conrad Hackett & David McClendon, Pew Research Center, "Christians remain world's largest religious group, but they are declining in Europe," April 5, 2017, http://www.pewresearch.org/fact-tank/2017/04/05/christians-remain-worlds-largest-religious-group-but-they-are-declining-in-europe/, accessed January 4, 2019.

# NOTES

# [ NOTES ]

# [ NOTES ]

# [ NOTES ]

# [ NOTES ]

# NOTES

_____

_____

_____

_____

_____

_____

_____

_____

_____

_____

_____

_____

_____